AN AUSTRALIAN CHILD'S VIEW OF THE SECOND WORLD WAR

by

GEOFFREY RICKARBY OAM

AN AUSTRALIAN CHILD'S VIEW OF THE SECOND WORLD WAR

Copyright © 2025

Published by
Gooragang Publications
ABN 77 845 063 813

ISBN 978-0-6453599-2-3

This book is copyright. Except for private study, research, criticism or reviews as permitted under the Copyright Act. No part of this book may be reproduced, stored in a retrieval system, or transmitted in any form by any means without prior written permission. Enquires should be to the publisher.

For the family

INTRODUCTION

A young child's viewpoint of The Second World War seen from a Melbourne suburb: Tooronga, Victoria, Australia.

This account arose from my sister Margaret's intense interest in family history, and specifically, around the time of her birth at this pivot of world history. She was born on August the 4th of 1939, and this became sufficient an issue for her, that suggesting/persuading her elder brother to write about how it happened – and happened again. She wanted to know what this meant for her family at 6 Creswick St, until he did start to write it down, and thus developed his own interest that also grew.

Considering this writing started in January 2nd 2010, this is reasonable in that I have had more time to do it.

We lived at 6 Creswick St Tooronga with our parents Reginald Fabian Rickarby and Freda Elizabeth Rickarby (nee Hartley). I was born in Camberwell on February 18th 1934; Margaret on August 4th 1939. We had no other siblings. This area is about eight kilometres South-east of central Melbourne.

The account will bring to the reader a viewpoint of the social changes at home and at school that we experienced. They are naïve and quite indirect. They become more direct when there were explanations from parents, and, listening in to parents' discussions, particularly when they were visited by my father's elder brother 'Uncle Basil' (Gordon Basil Rickarby). It is from all three that I developed opinions I trusted, although the media of the time plays a direct and significant role.

While two of our mother's aunts and their families also lived in Creswick Street, all four of our grandparents were dead. Both parent's families of that generation had moved to Western Australia following 'the gold' in the eighteen nineties, Reg's father Fred as a barrister and Freda's father George (with his brothers) to run their own mine. Both fathers had to return to Victoria with terminal illness.

Reg and Freda met at Ivanhoe Victoria in the twenties and married in 1933. Freda's grandparents were immersed in the social life of Ivanhoe, where grandfather Fred Skead taught ballroom dancing with the help of his seven daughters (embroidered ball gowns.) They were involved with the Caledonian society, and Lol Skead was a soprano entertainer. When Nellie and Midgie married, they moved to Tooronga.

So Freda's relatives were already at Tooronga, and were part of a syndicate that built the tennis-courts behind the Eastern side of the street. They had become a focus for my parents and my father was able to get support to take them over.

The qualities of my memory are quite different and vary from a those of a nearly five-year-old to a rapid reading eleven-year-old in Year 7 during 1945. I have been aware throughout that the form will change, and even the style of writing, yet this is necessary because such change is a theme in itself.

Reg and Freda Rickarby

1939

1939

This is the year when I settled to go to school regularly, just before I turned five. They had tried sending me during 1938, but, on the second morning, I had strongly resisted going and they accepted this.

The first event in my memory of 1939 was of the extreme heat and the dramatic bushfires of January 13th. It was referred to throughout my childhood as Black Friday. We had been for a number of holidays to Uncle Basil's 'shack' at Christmas Hills only a couple of miles from where my great-grandparents – (father's mother's side) settled in the 1850s, and where my great uncle and aunt (Charlie and Jess Young) lived.

Fred Lee and me on my first day of Gardiner Central School

My parents were worried about the people there during the firestorm, but we knew Uncle Basil wasn't there, as his main home was in Melbourne. Basil and Reg had spent the Xmas holidays clearing trees around the three-room shack below the peak of the Skyline Rd hill. This area is on the West side of The Yarra Valley and quite close to Melbourne.

My father said the fires were going faster than cars, and lots of people couldn't get away and were being killed. Even though the fires were more than ten miles away, the smoke covered all of the sky, and it seemed dark, but my father took me into the backyard to show me how you could see the sun faintly through the smoke — it was a rusty colour. Later in the year we were to drive through the burnt country and see all the chimneys standing among the ashes for the last part of the journey. Uncle Charlie's place near the creek survived; Uncle Basil's shack did not; I saw its ruins a few years later with a gum tree sapling growing up through a rusty iron bed frame.

A couple of weeks later, as had happened the previous year, I was taken to school by my cousin Fred Lee (my mother's first cousin) who was about seven years older than me.

In a South-Eastern suburb of Melbourne, Gardiner Central School catered to the kindergarten ('the bubs') and grades 1 to 6, and also to Form 1 and Form 2 of Secondary School. These two years accepted children from other primary schools.

My mother walked us across two of our tennis courts to the back gate, and we walked along the lane to Malvern Road, and then one and a half blocks to Osborne Avenue on its other side, and then another block until we came to the school: two story, red-brick: the High School part was upstairs, and I would see Fred going up and down the rusty external iron stair case.

There were two lady teachers who lined us up. I was dressed in white shirt and navy-blue short trousers that came to just above my knees, with a leather school bag on my back. Then I had navy-blue woollen socks with two white bands with black boots. It took a long time to get into them that morning. I could not tie my own laces. My family believed in boots, and I was often wishing I had school shoes like most of the other children. I heard that they would "get weak ankles".

Our two-bedroom home at 6 Creswick St, Tooronga had six tennis courts and a large pavilion behind us and many of the houses on our side of the street. They abutted to our rear fence. My father, with the support of his friend Joseph Justins was buying this property, while keeping up his job at the Newport railways workshop in a staff role. He was a leading hand fitter and turner.

These days, Google Earth now shows our home and courts site as uniform roof top for the block of twenty-seven apartments – single storey.

Sometimes I was taken to 'The Pictures' at this age. One film that affected me for years until I realised the connection, was the severe fire in a film about Gaugin in Tahiti, the other was a funny film called The Great Dictator, even though I didn't know what satirical aspects meant, I was completely aware how they were making fun of Hitler, and Charlie Chaplin was already familiar to me from all 'the shorts' I'd seen of him. I'd heard about Hitler often because the adults talked about him nearly all the time.

Looking at the screen, I was frightened more by cartoons that made impossible things happen or ran straight at your face. I was most disturbed by a baby called 'Baby Dumpling' crawling out on a window ledge of a multi-story building. I was horrified and didn't understand why everybody was laughing. Dagwood and Blondie were also to become regular comic strips in the newspapers.

Also, I didn't take too well to babysitters, specifically Aunty Nell Smitten, who wouldn't do it again because I kept repeatedly asking when 'They' were coming home and going to the door; It kept her away, and I guess that's why I saw a few films at that age.

Starting school for the second time, I was not as confused as previously, and listening to the teachers was much easier, and I could understand what was expected of me. I lined up past my own peg where my school bag would hang. One thing I noticed everywhere, was that any movable object had G R imprinted on it in big black letters. It seemed strange or important that everything had my initials on it. It took some explanation to me that week to understand that George Rex meant King George VI and Rex was a Latin word for King and that they all belonged to him.

I remembered names very well at that time. My teacher was called Mr Cullen. He was a kind man and very encouraging. I knew my numbers and letters, but the hardest thing for me was to write my letters well. There were blue lines for the body of the letter, and then there were red lines for a high loop - then another red line where the bottom loop should go; so a letter like 'f' would go up and down to both red lines. My lines were always a bit shaky and irregular. The teachers were never happy with my writing and they talked about how people with good writing would get good jobs when they grew up. The grown-ups often talked about 'good jobs'.

With numbers, I was excited about learning to add them together, and inherently knew this was very important. It seemed a very long day at school, but when I was a bit older, or somebody would go with me, I was able to go home for lunchtimes and return for afternoon school.

The eighteenth of February was my fifth birthday. I had a birthday party, and I would get very excited at this. My mother's friends would come, as well as some younger cousins and one of her friend's nieces and some children from Creswick St.

> *It is important to say that while Creswick St had twenty-six houses and went between the No 7 Malvern Road tramline and the railway line near Tooronga Station and was in every way an ordinary street in the middle-class area of the Higgins electorate, it was, unbeknown to almost all of its inhabitants, a pivotal place in the Second World War. This is because the shop on the city side corner of Malvern Road, and the dwelling above and behind it, was a used furniture shop kept by a Mr Hall. One of Mr Hall's sons, was a senior Australian Government official who was assigned full time to a new job, and what better place would there be for Australia's first intelligence service but above a furniture shop in the suburbs? ASIO was born there, although it was not officially named or outed until Mr Chifley announced it after the war was over.*

On the other corner of Creswick St from Mr Hall's furniture shop, was a dairy belonging to Bob and Phyllis Pollock; (Bob from Scotland and Phyl a Londoner) there was a small house in between, then a lane at the first dogleg, then our house: it was built fairly cheaply just before The Depression a decade earlier. It was plastered on lathes with a rough render of cement and charcoal and had two bedrooms.

Across Malvern Road from Mr Hall's shop was the yard where all the dairy horses were kept to deliver the milk during the night. Horses were used totally to deliver milk, bread, soft drinks, ice and by 'the bottle-o', and large draught horses were used by the Malvern City Council for repairs and rubbish collection. While most houses were connected to the sewer, 'the night cart' would still go up the back lanes to the few houses that were not connected. Two other houses in our street were occupied by two of my mother's aunts and their families. I knew they were two of my late grandmother's six sisters; Aunty Midge Lee at No 10 on our side, and Aunty Nell Smitten on the opposite side in No 11.

At this time the six tennis courts were going well. The soft-drink cart would come regularly to deliver the soft drinks we would sell to the tennis players. I would find milk thistles for the horses and gingerly offer them, keeping well away from their teeth.

I would watch the tennis and knew that various teams were playing each other, and they had a flagpole and would raise various flags. The scores confused me as they would call "forty-fif" and "juice". (I was sure for many years there was no 'D' in it, and had no idea what it meant outside its scoring significance.) During the week there were various social clubs playing, but not on all six courts. I was aware of the courts getting cracks in them, and my father worrying about this as the mixture of asphalt and sawdust they were surfaced with, was not doing what he expected it to do.

Our garden looked good and I knew the names of all the roses; we had a cleaning lady who came to help my mother and we went to 'the talkies' at the local 'picture theatre', and I can still experience my fear of some of the cartoons.

Being obsessed with trains was a core preoccupation, as I knew every set of points between Tooronga and Flinders St, but I was horrified by some of the films about trains where an accident was about to happen, and particularly the lady tied to the railway track.

I frequently heard my parents talking about the Great War of 1914-1918, where my mother's young Uncle Charlie (Skead) had been killed in Flanders.

The tennis courts, Reg is at the net looking back at Joe Justins.

There were quite a few films with soldiers fighting between trenches, and machine guns. My mother explained how my Aunty Cis had Lober nephews fighting on one side and her brother on the other. (Alice Maud Mary Lober nee Skead, the childless great-aunt who importantly stood in as a grandmother)

There was a strong sense of this earlier war and 'The Depression' among the adults' talk, and I always knew these two events were the big things they thought about often, although, from their talk, The Depression was the disaster that might most likely come again. I worried that I would be possibly in trench warfare like that when I grew up, but defended by thinking that was so far away.

One day later in the year, Mr Cullen was giving a few of us some single figure sums to do in one part of the class, and he put some zeros in the sums. Two of us could do it every time. The other was a girl whose parents had recently arrived from Europe, and who was some weeks younger than me. We were told their father had to escape from the Nazis in Germany, and they had come to Australia with their two daughters to be safe. Her name was Susie Loewe. As a result of this she and I were told we were going into the First Grade in the middle of the Year.

At this time, we were hearing about the Jewish people in Germany having things written on their shops and being bashed. My mother said they were escaping to other countries, and they wanted to get a long way from Germany. Some countries would take them, and other countries would not.

The First-Grade teacher was a Miss Jenkins who was more concerned about my handwriting. She looked severe, but she was never 'crabby', yet she looked very old. I understood that 'Miss' meant they were not married and that married teachers left work and looked after their husband and children. My mother explained to me that there were a lot of women who were engaged to a soldier of the First World War, but he was killed in action, and that so many had been killed that there were not enough husbands to go around. She said that some of these women were very sad.

During this time, I was introduced to the idea of our family having a new baby, by counting my pennies into piles to see if I had enough money towards a new baby for the family. When I counted my stacks optimistically, my father pointed out that I did not have twelve pennies to each pile and that half pennies (pronounced hayp'nee) were just that. I learnt from that, but nothing about babies and their origins, and like a large proportion of children in those times kept grossly ignorant (even during later childhood) of the facts of life, to an extent that would be implausible to a 21st Century child.

At various times my mother's unmarried brother, Uncle Frank HARTLEY would be home from the navy. He had been in the navy since 1929. My mother thought it had been

Frank Hartley, my mother's brother.

a good career for him. He would bring me numerous toys, some of them elaborate and interesting, and I was aware he thought I didn't value them or 'look after' them.

I had numerous toys including a Hornby train set that I valued more than the others. Also, I had a car that I could sit in which had a functional steering wheel and a bicycle chain drive from the pedals.

> Even today more than 85 years later, I think my driving skills were enhanced by this early experience, as I drove around our place and in Creswick Street, even sometimes around the Malvern Rd corner without leaving the footpath.

We were hearing a lot about Hitler. He was Germany's dictator and the boss of the Nazis, and people were worried about him. I associated the word 'Nazi' with 'nasty'. I was also hearing on the news about a man called Chamberlain and a place called Czechoslovakia that I knew was a country. My father was teaching me to play chess and he would say "Check!." That confused me with the people who lived in Czechoslovakia.

I was taught about maps and could find countries on them at a very early age. I did not understand that to a five-year-old such names came through as themes accompanied by the moods they created in the adults around them. Many words in the next couple of years would have this effect, such as 'Vichy' and 'Quisling', where the word meant nothing but the feeling did.

Then I suddenly knew that Uncle Frank was getting married quite soon. I most remember the visit by his fiancée Gwen and her parents, Mr and Mrs Cadd. I thought it was a strange name as I knew what the word 'cad' meant generally. I thought how beautiful Aunty Gwen was; to a child there was a sense of her being young, happy and outgoing, with a great smile and frizzy blonde hair, and when I was older, I realised it was the real thing. It didn't dawn on me why my father was groomsman at the wedding and my mother didn't go. In a few weeks' time I found out, but still didn't make the connection.

Because shortly after, in early August (4th), instead of my mother waking me, it was my father.

He told me I had a new baby sister, and that my mother was at the hospital where I had been born, called Seskinore, in South Camberwell, previously a large two-story home on the high side of Burke Road. In Melbourne, August is a time of cold miserable weather only broken by bulbs and blossom.

My father dressed me and said I would be able to go and see Mum and the new baby soon, but I was to go and stay with Aunty Midge (Florence Lee, nee Skead, Fred's mother) who lived two doors away on our side of Creswick St. Uncle 'Dicky Lee' had the local wood-yard and 'hay and corn store' in Malvern Road next to the bank.

In some ways this was a time of celebration, and the separation was explicable and well tolerated by me. Aunty Midge had delicious honey and always had fresh bread. I still remember an accurate internal plan of her house, which was a solid brick Federation style, almost twice the size of our house.

My sister was called Margaret Anne. I knew she was 5 pounds 2 ounces and that was quite small. I had seen many photos of the two princesses and I knew the younger one was Princess Margaret; I identified my mother with Queen Elizabeth, later 'Queen Mother' because she was the same size and shape, with similar hair, and was also the mother of two children.

There were visits to the hospital, and I was surprised how small a baby my new sister was. After two weeks she came home with my mother, and then I was preoccupied with the change in routine. I can remember being very surprised by my mother breast feeding her, and this was explained to me in a straightforward direct manner. Margaret's bath time became the time when the relatives would come to look — particularly Fred's older sisters Nance and Alison.

The baby was so much the foreground that although 'Poland' was often repeated and comparisons with Czechoslovakia, over and over on the wireless and by adults; it meant nothing to me except being familiar with all the names.

But very shortly after this: when the family was all together after the 'lying in period' at the hospital, my parents together told me very seriously that the Germans had gone to war again after only twenty years, and because Hitler's armies had gone into Poland, and England had declared war, Australia was at war too. I can remember my father saying, "It's only twenty years since the last one finished."

I can still remember being told that in the previous war, Hitler had only been a corporal. I heard my mother telling my father how worried she was that Uncle Frank would go to the war in a ship very quickly. My father did not go because he was in his "late thirties", and I will tell later of my two trips to his work to see what he did, including about his connections to the war.

The next week my teenage cousin Shirley (Shirley Fernee) arrived from Winkie in the Upper Murray Region of South Australia to be looked after because she had 'the Murray Cough'. She had come about three years earlier with 'The Murray Pox' and given me Chicken Pox. Shirley was the daughter of the youngest of my grandmother's six sisters - Aunty Bess. This 'cough' was a disaster as both my new baby sister and I came down with Whooping Cough.

I can remember coughing and coughing and not able to stop until I was sick. But the baby was much worse; she would vomit repeatedly in huge streams. The family's fear for my sister became mine too, and it overrode any concern for myself – but I was more secure staying home from school. I can remember a scene of my mother coming into the dining room with the baby and a sudden vomit shooting from the baby's mouth like a hose. My mother said she often had to put her finger into the baby's throat to pull out thick masses of mucous.

My mother appeared, what I would call today, distressed and distraught.

My father went to his job with the railways six days a week, and friends had to help with the Tennis Courts. I had to stay home from school. The doctor came and there were little bottles of medicine and I listened to my parents talking. I knew they were very angry as to why we became so sick, and about what my mother's relatives would want her to do. My parents were frightened badly that our baby would die.

I also knew that Auntie Olive and Uncle Tom Kirkham had two children, and they didn't have them now because they had died of pneumonia, and that I wasn't allowed out to play with other children, because there was a lot of Polio around and you had to live in 'an iron lung' at a place called Fairfield if you 'got Polio'

> Having been a GP through a series of whooping cough epidemics in the fifties and sixties, I now know that the breast feeding well established was what saved Margaret. In the thirties there were no antibiotics to treat complications and artificial feeding was not sophisticated.

That Spring seemed very long. I went back to school and was rapidly learning to read. At this time, I knew that my mother was the greater family's dressmaker, everything from wedding dresses and their elaborate veils, to baby clothes. As well, Aunty Nell (at the price of tolerable condescension from her) who was known to be 'good at making trousers', would make me a suit to have as my 'good clothes'. In those days 'little boys' did not wear underpants beneath their trousers. These suit trousers were big, rough, irritating and prickly, and the double-breasted coat was tight and hot and constricting, and I was threatened that I was not to get it dirty: the main cause of me being in trouble as a child.

My parents subscribed to a weekly paper called Smith's Weekly, that had many cartoons in it, many of them portraying Hitler, who was always unmistakable. I was confused between Hermann and Musso, but the latter had a distinctive lower face and neck. In that form they were not frightening, but it was very frightening to think of being a soldier. I was looking through all the newspapers my father brought home, mostly the Melbourne Sun from the morning and The Herald in the evening. I was attracted to maps and I already had a World Atlas with the British Empire countries shown in red. In all the newspapers, the maps would show with arrows which way the taking of territory was going, and there were bigger markings where there was an established front.

Me in the suit.

    I was miserable about this suit and would do anything to avoid being dressed in it. Sunday morning going to Sunday School in Malvern Rd, where Fred's sisters taught, was the most likely one.

    We went to Brighton Beach for a holiday at Christmas. I remember being very thrilled at finding the Adventures of Blinky Bill by Dorothy Wall in my pillowcase on Christmas morning. We were in a converted garage that was let at that season.

    While my mother read it to me, I was impatient to see what happened next, and found I could read most of it, but would ask about some of the words. We were out walking with the pram and met a couple of nuns, and one asked if she could have a hold of the baby.

Margaret screamed loudly for her five months of age. My mother quickly took her back and the nuns were apologetic and said that she must have had the metal cross stuck into her. When my father heard this story, he was very angry.

We always ate a lot of fresh fish when we were on such a holiday as it was caught locally. I also remember there seemed to be a huge shock around the district as people talked about a man, diving from Brighton Beach pier, was taken by a large shark.

This actually happened in 1930, but people talked about it as though it was that week.

1940

I distinctly remember New Year's Day 1940, as we went further down The Bay to Black Rock. There were high cliffs over the beach with a lot of coastal scrub still conserved. An old ship had been sunk off the beach as a breakwater and my father said that 'wags' had been out to it and painted 1940 on the side earlier in the day. The ramps down to the beach were very steep but I found that I could walk down them and up them, as I had been quite fearful of even insignificant heights when I was younger.

My mother would take Margaret to the Baby Health Centre in Malvern; sometimes we would go on the tram, but other times we would walk. She would be very upset that the Sister (triple certificate nurse at the baby health centre) would be very cross that Margaret wasn't gaining weight and this reduced her to tears on a number of occasions. However, Margaret's chest was recovering well and the dry summer was probably helping it.

In the December at school, after a film had been shown to us, the number 75 had appeared on it. I had said, "That's three quarters of a hundred."

The teachers had also been appealing for anything, particularly old pots and balls of foil because the government needed it for aeroplanes. It was important for the war. I took this on board in detail and particularly looked around vacant lots and other places where we children would play. They actually gave me an award on a big piece of paper. Somehow it got lost.

When School returned, I was into Second Grade, and learnt later that the fraction had decided it. There were quite a few children much older than Susie and I, including Juneshi Amano. Juneshi's parents were here from Japan only recently and his father was 'a businessman.' I had seen Juneshi a few times in the street as he lived between my home and the Railway Station. He was friends with two of the older boys, one of whom had a reputation of being very tough.

There were a few temporary young teachers at the beginning of the year, one of whom hit me across the knuckles with a ruler. But Miss Newton arrived and we settled for the year. There were only two term holidays of a week each throughout the year. I was still unable to tie up my own bootlaces and wanted to have shoes like the other children, but my mother still had ideas about strong straight legs.

On my birthday, my mother told me that we wouldn't be having a birthday party this year. She said that because many of the young men were 'joining up' and people weren't available to play tennis as much as they used to, and we were not getting as much money, and because we were paying for the tennis-courts we had to be very careful of how much money we spent.

Our house-cleaning lady had stopped. Instead of a party, my mother took me to Hall's Book Store in Flinders Lane (not the same Hall) central Melbourne and gave me the choice of books I might want to read. I bought four and read them to myself: one was the adventures of Robin Hood; another was a Book of Saints.

It was about this time that I was taken to 'the pictures' to see a film that I watched right through. It had a lasting impression. It was Forty Thousand Horsemen that showed the Australian Horsemen at war in the Desert during World War One. It added to my disquiet about warfare, with artillery and machine guns fully involved. I was too young to understand the Charge at Beersheba, let alone its implications.

Every Sunday I was going to Sunday School. My cousins first took me when I was very small: Nance, one of Fred's older sisters was a teacher, or I was collected at the front gate by a Miss Sheridan who brought a whole group of children with her, all holding each other's hands. I absorbed all the bible stories totally. Indeed, before this account starts, I had complained about a repeat of 'Moses and the Bulrushes', and I was challenged to tell it myself — which I did in sequence and detail.

My mother talked about The Maginot Line and why it was going to stop the Germans and keep everybody safe. She explained that the French had built up a line of forts and defences between France and Germany that even tanks couldn't get through. She showed me where it was on the map.

However, things were not so good at home. When he was younger, my father had a poultry farm, and when the Depression came, eggs became worthless, and he had to leave it and lose it; now, a similar situation had come along, and the Tennis Courts looked as if they would go the same way. The payments still had to be made; the tennis players had gone.

Miss Newton distributed a small booklet about life in Japan. It was about the family of a little girl called Akiku. I read it quickly. It was an orderly simple life with a lot of blossoms and neat gardens. It fostered some bad behaviour in the playground, as some of the more hostile children would say Akiku and then do just that with their foot, and then laugh.

Marg and me 1940

My mother said Japan was very crowded and a terrible place for earthquakes; then described such quakes graphically. I had fearful preoccupations with earthquakes and volcanoes as my mother seemed to know a great deal about Vesuvius and Pompeii and talked about it to me in detail.

I tried to talk to Juneshi on one occasion and was asking him about something Japanese, and he became angry at the word and tried to hit me. I ran.

Then, towards the middle of the year, the Germans went into Holland and Belgium quickly, and then across an area of Belgium that had been thought unlikely, straight into the top corner of France. The Maginot Line was bypassed. My parents showed me on the maps and from then on, I would follow all the maps of the war. I pored over atlases, and knew the names of many cities and countries that now don't exist or have been called something else.

Our wireless, a large brown piece of furniture around which I had crawled in infancy, had always been much taller than me, was turned on for every news. What followed during that May were defeats followed by routs. It led to Dunkirk. It was held up by some churches as a miracle, as the French and English armies escaped across the English Channel in hundreds of little boats, while the waves stayed still and a fog hid them. There was a constant message in my early 'religious instruction' that religious belief was closely tied to miracles.

I was dealing with my fear of heights by jumping off a table, and then, from a chair on top of a table that succeeded once, but the second time, my hand hit the ground first. This meant being taken to the Alfred Hospital. It was a huge old brick building. I was in a lot of pain: both bones were broken and my arm was an odd shape. The nurses put me on a trolley and took me away. My crying increased to very loud bawling. This attracted the attention of an older nurse who came and scolded me severely, but I kept bawling loudly. I wanted my mother and I didn't know what was going to happen. An older nurse with an fancy uniform came and told me very sternly to stop behaving badly as it was upsetting people. I continued. It seemed to go on for a long time, until a man came and put a mask over my face and the fumes spread in my head.

Me, 6 years and 3 months old, May 1940

I woke on a trolley with my arm in plaster almost to the top.

My arm was hurting, but not as badly as before. I was told we were going home. I don't remember how we got home. I did not go back to school for the six weeks before the plaster was removed. I was told it was 'set' while I was 'asleep'.

When I was in second year Medicine I was taught about Madelung's deformity as a traumatic consequence of injury - the growing plate at the lower end of the radius, where the radius was damaged and did not grow as the ulna did. It left me unable to straighten my elbow and particularly to have very limited rotation of my forearm. In 2019 there seems to be a variety of causes, and the 'eponymous naming' is mostly only used for the genetic type. But the description in 1952 accurately fits.

Margaret in her high chair waiting for lunch

As 1940 went on, I was to hear Winston Churchill on the radio and knew he was the new British Prime Minister because Neville Chamberlain had been 'weak and foolish'. Hitler had gone through Belgium and France so fast that there were widespread fears he would invade England very quickly. The wireless kept repeating Mr Churchill saying how they would fight everywhere - I specifically remembered 'the beaches' - and 'never surrender'. At this time Hitler's Dorniers and Messerschmitts were coming over England to get ready for an invasion. I could say 'Messerschmitts' crisply, but not Dorniers, and so could every other boy; it was among the most used words.

The British Air-force had been strong and we were told Germany couldn't invade while the RAF was able to attack them from the air. The Hurricanes and later the Spitfires had 'dogfights' with the German planes and attacked them at every opportunity, although many pilots were killed. This battle went on for many weeks until the Germans were losing so many planes and airmen that they had to give up. This left everybody in awe of the men and the planes - we knew that many Australians were there flying them. It was only later that I was to know it was called The Battle of Britain.

I understood that the Italians had come into the war too, because I knew that ships now had to go around The Cape of Good Hope because the Italians could stop them going by the Suez Canal. I knew the geography of this and could point out where Mussolini was having his wars in Ethiopia.

My mother started getting together food parcels for England. Her family from her mother's side, had been in Australia for five generations, and, on her father's side for three, but those two great-grandparents had been a 'child convict' from Leeds and an orphaned girl from Württemberg, so my mother adopted Phyl and Bobby Pollock's relations (Phyl's sister, the Byl family of Wimbledon) as if her own, and sent food parcels regularly.

Reg, Margaret and me with my car

They particularly valued foods with a fatty content as they were deprived of meat and butter. Beef dripping was highly prized. Some of the parcels arrived, but others did not, as we were told that a large number of ships making this run were torpedoed by U-boats.

My mother sewed each parcel into a cloth cover. and then carefully addressed it in block letters. She sent similar parcels to Uncle Frank. We knew his ship was going overseas and we later learned it was posted to the Mediterranean area. He had been promoted to Petty Officer.

At this time the tennis courts were now only used one day a week by the ladies from 3AW who only used one court. My father had now built two fowl pens and reorganised part of the back garden to grow vegetables. I would grow radishes and carrots, and I would eat the peas in their shells straight off the plant, and similarly young beans.

Because our resources were needed by the forces, many things were rationed: meat, butter and tea were the main ones. Coffee was unthinkable, but people could buy an artificial coffee: essence of chicory. Fuel was strictly rationed, but as we did not have a car, this was not a big issue, although I knew my father had some ration coupons because he traded them with a friend Bob White who would later take us in his car on some holidays.

I had to pass the local petrol pump on my way to school. The vehicles would come to the kerbside (then we called it 'the gutter' but did not use 'gutter' for roof plumbing as other states of the country) where the pump was hard by. The garage man would pump the petrol up into a clear vessel above; it had gallons marked on the side. After he was paid for it, the man would turn on the hose and the petrol flowed down into the fuel tank. It had a distinctive odour, that when dilute was quite pleasant and unmistakable, but if your nose was too near, it was nasty like the anaesthetic.

One big thing about the era was the materials. While 'perspex' was something new being talked about, 'bakelite' was a ceramic material that was a non-conductor of electricity and had been around for some time. At school the following year, I was going to be allowed to write in ink and each desk had two ceramic ink-wells.

Plastics and the term 'plastic' were still some four or five years from entering the language. However, every child was familiar with the unfired clay product for modelling called plasticine. Jute was another commonly used material for bags, particularly those containing potatoes or briquettes. Asbestos was used for insulation and to make building materials that needed a binder such as cement sheeting, and, in the kitchen - I know that for our coal-gas stove we had a three-part asbestos mat that would spread the gas flame without melting, so that three pots could be put on the one flame.

Coal gas in Melbourne contained carbon monoxide and was very dangerous and talked about with some anxiety by adults. (I was to tell the teacher about 'carbon bonoxide') Wood was used much more widely. Butter always came from the wholesaler in a large cubic box and the grocer had to cut into this huge cube of butter with wooden paddles and weigh it in pounds and ounces.

It is ironic that the parents today will talk with such anxiety now about asbestos, while carbon monoxide is only talked about as a danger in closed garages and heaters in closed rooms, but, as a less common cause of environmental death.

One day just before the summer holidays in December, Miss Newton announced that Juneshi would be leaving us to go back to Japan. A few days later his mother arrived at the school to take him home for the last time. She brought a series of kits of varied coloured pencils for the students to use at school. Through Miss Newton, she thanked us for giving Juneshi a kind and understanding year at school. (If she only knew it, because he was an ally of Georgie Johnson; nobody would have challenged him in any manner.) My parents and Uncle Basil were interested in why they were going home.

My cousin Win (Aunty Myra's daughter from Ultimo near Swan Hill) was there for Christmas 1940. She would kill one of 'the chooks' with an axe. I didn't watch that bit, but I did watch her taking the feathers off and taking its innards out. This included an egg, as if ready to be laid. She had stayed with us before for quite some time and was an expert at this, as they often did it on the farm at home. She was about 17 and worked as a live-in maid at one of the local doctor's homes. She was also my mother's first cousin. Her younger sister Myra was to come down to town also, and I was going to be able to sleep in the 'sleep out', a room made on our back verandah, by enclosing it.

Eating poultry was an ultimate Christmas treat. I can still taste its rich flavour in a manner that contrasts immensely with modern 'chickens'. (In the forties the word 'chicken' was only used to described the fluffy baby, and 'chicken' as a generic term was considered as a strange Americanism) and my mother made the stuffing from bread and herbs and onions. I didn't like onions, but cooked tomato and pumpkin were worse. Christmas time was also a time of rich Christmas cake and Christmas pudding in which were tossed quite a few coins all made of silver, so one kept eating pudding. I remember eating some of Aunty Nell's pudding after Christmas and found a shilling. I ignored her suggestion to put it back for next year.

Mothers did a lot of baking, and sponges and scones were cooked frequently. Each aunt, or the mothers of friends had very distinct scones and sponges. The bakery at the corner of the street did pies, pasties (as Cornish miners used) and sausage rolls, but each family bought flour and baked, but their pies were usually large and for the family. Steak and kidney pie or pudding was a recurrent one. I liked the latter best but would always pick the kidney out of it before eating.

We were still gatherers, in that, at the right time, we would pick wild blackberries or mushrooms. I loved the blackberry jam but refused mushrooms at that age.

My father hated gravy, so our meals were very simple most of the time. Every day we would have meat, either steak or a lamb chop (steak was rationed more than lamb chops) with potatoes, often mashed, and, in season, new potatoes with butter, after you took off the fine skin; and then one or two other vegetables, such as beans, peas, cauliflower or carrots. Mostly the meats were grilled under the gas 'griller'. (This familiar word is now totally unacceptable to modern software). Chicken at special occasions (we always killed our own bird) would be roasted if young (a 'rooster') or boiled if it was an old one. Of a Sunday lunch we would have a roast that was either a leg-of-lamb or a rolled-up beef roast that I disliked because of all the fat in it. We would have such deserts as preserved fruit with cream. Cream was not expensive, and our milk also came with a layer of cream making up about 2 inches as the top of the milk-bottle that had a lid made of waxed cardboard pressed on at its wide top.

My mother also made a variety of desserts, many of which were apple based — also served with whipped cream. I learnt to do the whipping with a winding handle on the side of the whipper, although my mother would use a whipper with a wire coil and a wooden handle.

Salads were frequent; her potato salad was very tasty, with potatoes chopped small and a tiny amount of chopped cooked bacon and chopped white celery and even walnut pieces, also her spiced egg toast and the treat 'raspberry and red-current pie' in season. I realised as an adult that these foods had come from her grandmother who came as an orphan from Wurttemburg in the 1850s, or from Aunty Cis's mother-in law.

> *Imagine my surprise to have my mother's potato salad dished up to me at a Frieberg in Breslau restaurant in the 1980s.*

As a young child, I was told we could not grow celery in our garden because it needed a special farm where the celery was grown in trenches to keep the light from the stalks.

I would eat celery again if it was of the quality of my childhood.

Our apple trees were attacked by codling-moth. but we always seemed to have many apples because Uncle Dick Lee had a farm in the country with many fruit trees in his orchard, and kept pigs as well that lived in the mud and ate any sort of food they were given. We could get to it by train because we caught the train at Tooronga, and arrive at the edge of greater Melbourne at East Malvern. Then there was a little old single carriage train that would go all the way through the bush and farms to Glen Waverley. At one place there were streets and kerbs but no houses. My mother explained that they nearly built houses, but then The Depression happened. We would get off the train at a station called Syndal and walk a short distance to the farm.

Charlie Lewis and I recently drove from his home nearby to have a look at this area; old suburbia. I knew the direction from the lie of the land and we found ourselves right where it was; fifty-year-old brick homes. But we were in the right place: Lee Street.

We always had raisins and nuts or dates around the house for snacks, but as the war went on, the dates were not obtainable. Tinned salmon stopped completely; my mother said that Barney, our half Persian cat, missed it the most because he would clean out the tins.

Christmas went on, but Boxing Day was also a very big day at our house, as this day in 1940 my mother would turn thirty-six. Margaret would sit in her highchair at the extension table opposite her, that when contracted, was almost round, and somebody would be there to offer her another spoonful of food. She was said to have a savoury taste and would not eat a lot of sweet food or desert. Everybody was still worried about her weight. As an older child, walnut and Vegemite sandwiches were to be her favourite

Geoffrey Rickarby 1940

Me in the 1940 Gardiner Central School class photo

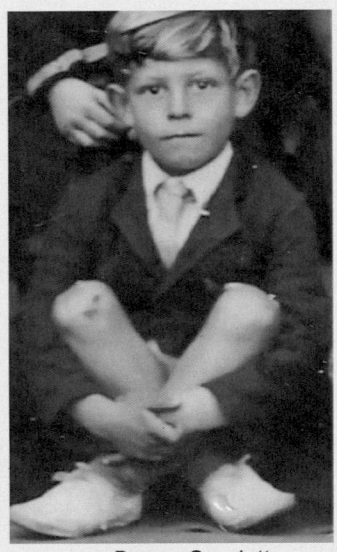

Donny Scarlett

Margaret Davis

Donny, Margaret and Susie, friends and classmates through school.

Susie Loewe

1941

When the New Year came, there were stories about the Australian soldiers in the Middle East and North Africa, particularly holding on to Tobruk. Very early that year, Hitler sent a general called Rommel to command the Afrika Korps, because English and Australian forces had been doing well against the Italians, and had taken thousands of Italian prisoners, and so German soldiers were required to fight in the desert.

In 1941, I commenced school in the last days of January. I was soon to be seven. By now I would always make my way independently to school, with frequent repetitions from my mother about crossing Malvern Road. The cars started to look strange because some would have a platform attached to the rear bumper, on which was a cylinder about three foot high that would smoke. This was a 'gas producer' and the wood, charcoal or briquettes that were put in it would be heated and give off a gas that would run the car. However, at this stage they were a curiosity, but their owners didn't need petrol coupons.

Miss 'Denehee' (that is how we said it) my third-grade teacher looked even older than Miss Jenkins. My mother had heard she was a very good teacher. She had her good days and bad days. She too was interested in the war and the places where it was fought, and when she asked where some place was, she had to exclude me to get other people to answer. Then she got me to ask one of these questions daily. This went well for a couple of weeks until I asked where Hammerfest was. Nobody had any idea, and when I said it was the town closest to the North Pole, she was irritated by this. I'd thought it was important, but our session fizzled out after this.

I was to visit Arctic Norway in the early eighties and learn how they had fought the Germans steadily southward down that coast in the last year of the European War, but although I was close to Hammerfest at times, regretfully I didn't actually get there.

At least she would let me read when some of the lessons became repetitive. She was keen on spelling contests, but Susie and another girl called Margaret Davis would beat me at that.

The latter was to be in my class throughout primary school, and with the exception of the last four years of secondary school, that were unisex, she went through all six years of Medicine with me. She was noted for her fine neat needle work, so I was not surprised when she became a paediatric surgeon noted for her neat and precise work.

At this time, I was struggling to find enough to read. I reread various books including the Pooh Bear, Christopher Robin story versions of AA Milne. My mother had read me the first two books and their verse since before I could remember, and also a poetry collection she had in year 7 and 8. I looked at every book on my parent's bookcase, and my father had a Book of Myths that I would reread. A preference was the Norse myths about Loki, Thor and Odin. The first really long book I read was called Masterman Ready and then Treasure Island. I found it hard to believe all the frightening situations Jim Hawkins was in.

I was quite an anxious child around my seventh birthday. I knew the significance of being 21, and I knew that three sevens were 21. I was very anxious after the Sunday School children had gone to a special day at Sunday School where an evangelist lady was talking. Going to Heaven and Hell were very real issues to her, and only the people who did everything right got there. There was also a picture in the school corridor of volcanoes erupting.

Considering my mother's stories of Vesuvius and Pompeii, that focused my anxiety, I now know that fear of earthquakes and volcanoes was a useful defence against the anxieties sown by a supernaturalist religion and its frightening evangelists. I was later to understand why one of my daughters left a beautiful choir because they exposed her to such people.

At school we had religious instruction every week, but it was more like the story part of Sunday School. I had taken to reading The Bible at Sunday School because I could read it quickly, nothing else was available and boredom frequent.

I knew the British and Australians had captured a lot of places from the Italians in Libya the previous year, and I had already learned that the important one was Tobruk. It was in the middle of Libya on the Mediterranean coast. It was important for Rommel to capture it on his way to capture Cairo and the Suez Canal. My mother even had a book about the building of the Suez Canal and talked about its importance to England and Australia, and I would always listen to such interesting things she spoke about. I even tried to read the book.

Me, Margaret and dad, and that damned suit

Anyway, Rommel did everything he could to capture Tobruk, but the Australians made the old Italian fortress with all its tunnels and bomb shelters their own. The British still had some big guns there too. The Germans had big guns and Stukas too. Stukas were one of Hitler's secret weapons that were very big in the early part of the war, because they could drop their bomb very accurately when diving very low and fast.

But they couldn't beat the Australians out of Tobruk, and they held out there for over six months. During that time many Australian families were in anxiety for what would happen to their sons and husbands in Tobruk. Adults talked about it. The News on the radio talked about it.

My mother knew Uncle Frank was likely to be on a ship in that area, because she said, with places like Gibraltar and Malta being protected by our navy the Germans didn't have it all their way in The Mediterranean. The general feeling was one of pride that our soldiers were carrying their full weight of fighting in Africa.

I didn't realise until I was an adult and knew about other wars before and after World War 2, that this war was a much clearer moral call from all points of view than most of the others — moral conflict was not common and the voices of dissension were very quiet indeed, particularly for an outspoken country like ours.

I was highly attracted to Spitfires, as Donny Scarlett over the road (a laneway separated their house from Hall's back gate) was talking about them a great deal, and I saw pictures of their very sleek lines. He took a coloured one to school and we all marvelled at it. Films were being made about the air force battles of the war already, and we could go and absorb as much of that as we could see. Donny's brothers had all joined the services, one brother, Joe, was in the navy, and his eldest brother was in the army somewhere in the Islands. His older sisters were nurses, and from my greater family, Win's brother Ivan had joined the Air Force. My cousin Myra (Myra Smitten daughter of Aunty Nell nee Skead) from No 11 Creswick St - her fiancé Lindsay Tacon, had become a camouflage specialist.

One day I heard my father telling my mother that, "It is important to take him (me) to the workshops," ... so I would know it was important to get a really good job that wouldn't be like his workshops at Newport. During the following week, I was quite excited about going to work with him on the day. We were to go on the train. It was very early and the sun was rising. I wanted to see locomotives and liked complex rail-tracks with many points. I had never been on the short line to Williamstown previously and was alert to the stations, and what I could see of the other side of Melbourne. We got off at Newport.

The workshops were very old and dirty, big open buildings with high ceilings. There were rows of machines and they were all going when we got there. Many of them were shooting sparks out. Most of them had a fluid like dirty milk being squirted on the piece of metal, and I watched one closely and I knew it was cutting the part of a very big nut where the spanner would grip it.

I was among a group of machines that had a lot of things like potato bags in large squares. All of a sudden, they burst into very loud noises. I was suddenly afraid and jumped backwards moving very quickly to where I had entered the area, being careful not to run into anything. I was a very cautious child, and I knew intuitively that I would not be very good at anything the army did. But overall I was pleased with the day, and have thought since that he wanted to show his boy to the other people at work.

Writing this made me think of the day in 1956 when I became a doctor, he came home from work the next night in a merry mood because various ones had been celebrating for him all day. It makes me sad for him that his education went nowhere, as his father died when he was in primary school, and despite his brilliant father and paternal grandmother, let alone his maternal grandfather's diary, he was not to have the benefit of a good education or qualifications.

Mr Curtin was Australia's Prime Minister and in these unusual times; everybody seemed to think he was doing a good job, and I was aware that many people were surprised by this. I felt secure in Miss Denehy's class and took in everything taught, but was disappointed in her some years later when her version of the moon's phases was not correct and I had to revise my version of 'the cosmos'. There were some surprises that year: some daring young women wore long trousers called 'slacks'. One would drive the baker's horse to deliver the bread. She let me help her voluntarily, as I would put the bread on front-verandas. I realised that a skill behind this came from the horse who knew how to pace, and where to place the breadcart as the round developed.

There was a lot of discussion about women doing men's jobs, and would they give them back when the war was over? There was a sense that the war was going slowly, but that Hitler had not invaded England, and, as the year went on, Hitler not getting to Cairo, were very important, and that everybody thought the war would be over one day, but didn't know when. Yet there was a strong sense that Mr Churchill would be fighting until it was won completely.

Me, Margaret and dad, at Rye

Then, in the middle of the school year, when we had the fire alight in the front corner of the classroom, and the school's chimneys were smoking, and the white Melbourne frost took some hours of direct sunlight to melt, my parents were excited. "Hitler has invaded Russia!"

I could tell that this was not bad news to them at all. My mother knew a lot about Napoleon, particularly that if he had not invaded Russia, he might have won all his wars. She said that Napoleon had no idea how much worse the Russian Winter was compared with France. She told me how his armies were not only cold, but they got sick, they couldn't move around because everything froze, and so did their guns and horses.

She said that with so many of Hitler's armies in Russia, meant he couldn't use them in Africa and England, and that they would lose many of them. And it would mean that the Russians would be on 'our side'. I understood it was summer there at the time.

It was, as my father thought out loud: "Hitler's a fool." You could tell immediately that fools didn't win wars.

I was alarmed however by looking at the maps in the Sun or the Herald, and knew the Germans had taken a huge amount of Russian territory and were advancing on some of the great cities at the heart of Russia. We had morning newspapers and an evening newspaper that came out in a series of editions. Particularly on Saturday evening it was important to look at the 'Stop Press' done in red about halfway down the pane of the front page. It would have the final VFL football scores.

The boys who sold the papers were of two sorts, the ones who went to busy areas like the Tooronga Rd tram stop or The Regent Gardiner cinema (we called it 'the picture theatre" and wouldn't have understood the word 'cinema'), and the other boys that dropped the papers at houses. Such boys were called 'Herald boys'. In the morning, they would call, 'S'nage'n'argus' and in the evening, "Yee'a'errol"'. To get it authentic you need to imagine a ten-year-old, calling like a yodeller in a high pitched voice as he's jumped on the tram before it has stopped, and easily steps off as its starting to roll. My mother said, "Don't think you will ever be a Herald-boy." She said it crisply and left no doubt about the issue. The morning papers were 'The Sun', 'The Age' and 'Argus'.

By this time, I was reading The Sun and The Herald regularly, and The Australian Women's Weekly' and the 'Smith's Weekly, mentioned already. We didn't get the Women's Weekly, but invariably one would get copies to read when it was thrown out by somebody, or read it at one of the Aunt's places.

All that year The Axis (The News would talk about 'The Allies' and 'The Axis' confusing to a boy who knew what an axe was.) couldn't get the Australians out of Tobruk. And at the other front of the war there was terrible fighting. My mother explained that the Russians were using 'the scorched earth' policy where they destroyed everything that might be of value to the Germans Newsreels were saying that the weather was already a problem for the Germans, but that their armies were close to Leningrad and Moscow. But their winter was coming too. I knew there had been a whole war called the Crimean War, so that when the Germans took that part quickly, I thought they must be very strong. It looked like there were terrible things going to happen to everybody.

December 7th, 1941, was an ordinary early summer's day at Creswick St. That was because it was around midnight at the end of our day that things started to happen around Hawaii. The international dateline divides the two countries. So, it was already December the eighth when we hear the news in the morning. What we heard was catastrophic, that the 'American Fleet' was destroyed in Pearl Harbour by the Japanese.

The Japanese entering the war: even to my seven-year-old mind was something very frightening. It meant fears of bombing and invasion here in Australia. It meant that now the war was really starting, and closer to home. It was more than our pre-war tennis players fighting overseas and some of them being killed or taken prisoner; it would impinge more directly on Creswick St. My parents would go over the daily list of deaths repeatedly, although Stootsy (Royston) Snellgrove is the only name I can remember now. He survived.

This view was reinforced as all the relations and friends were discussing it with my parents; the repeated shock was how surprised and unprepared the Americans had been. We had no idea of how World War Two was to pivot on this week: that the German army in Russia was in a pitiful predicament as my mother's comments about Napoleon were understatements. The Germans hadn't taken Leningrad or Moscow; the slush was frozen, and it was more degrees below zero than I could imagine. And on the next day, I now know the Australians were quietly evacuated by sea from Tobruk, and despite Rommel's successes in the desert there were many battles he would have needed to win to take Cairo.

But as the third grade at Gardiner Central school was preparing to say goodbye to

Miss Denehy, news about Japan was all over the radio and newspapers. We heard about dreadful things they had been doing in China and that they had attacked Malaya already. My mother had huge confidence in the British in Malaya and their great fortress at Singapore where the British Navy was at strength. 'Britannia rules the waves', was something I had known before 'remembering' happened. It was like the red part of the map, and

American soldiers called out 'Hey Blondie!!', to Margaret.

Malaya was red.

There was talk about, 'everything from Japan' being, 'cheap and breaks easily' and about them going to use fireworks as weapons.

My mother knew about British battleships and how important they were. Australia was talking about the loss of their own, the 'Sydney', somewhere close to Australia. But suddenly, while we were hearing about Pearl Harbour, the Repulse was sunk by torpedoes.

She went on to talk about the Repulse and the Renown who were sister battleships, and when I heard that two had been sunk, I thought it was these two, until I read myself that the other one sunk was called The Prince of Wales and was an even bigger battleship, and that it had been done near Malaya. I knew the biggest most powerful battleship in the Royal Navy was HMS Hood. The Germans also had a massive battleship called

'The Tirpitz.' The Americans of course, I thought, had lost their battleships at Pearl Harbour earlier in the month. I heard people talking about various young men they knew being sent to Malaya and Singapore.

That Christmas my parents hired a house on the main Rd at Tootgarook near Rye on the Mornington peninsula. I can still remember having fears of supernatural events and was still disturbed by the dangers of abuse from the unknown supernatural pitfalls that might occur to me and my family. On the other view this holiday helped my ability to have detailed scenarios in my head, and my needing time to walk about privately to develop them. On the bush block of land there were interesting birds and some really strange lizards that I developed into a fantasy about a zoo with all sorts of Australian animals and birds.

There was the usual swimming and eating fresh fish, and it was good that my father was not working and he taught me to play cards and chess. At this stage Margaret was always sitting up to the table in her highchair and it was nice to have the four of us around the table together.

On this holiday we went on a bus trip up the small steep hill called Arthur's Seat.

It was the usual old bus ride where the bus driver 'double-de-clutches' with a lot of brm-brming, but we looked out above at all the places below and my father pointed out the You-Yangs down the other side of the bay, but my mother was upset, shaking and even crying. I only then learned that she was frightened of heights and a lot of other things as well. I didn't connect this with my own fearful childhood, but for the first time recognised that she was frightened when I was not.

On the other hand, this was a holiday from the war. While we got the newspaper once or twice, we weren't having it all the time. But the beach reserve was directly across the road and my mother repeatedly said how safe it was. I dived through very small waves while Margaret sat in the shallows with a big hat on.

1942

Going home from this holiday was memorable because, when we reached Caulfield Railway Station on the train, instead of going home on the Bourke Rd bus, we went home in a big taxi, one of those large pre-war American cars where you could feel 'the floating' over bumps on springs. I thought how wonderful it would be to have a car to be able to go where you wanted to. I hoped I would have a very good job one day, and that there wouldn't be another depression so that I would be able to have a car of my own. (The war didn't distract from the huge impact of The Depression — my father said correctly that it became much worse because the banks wouldn't lend any money.) It was now 1942.

We came home to constant talk of Singapore. Singapore was the great defendable fortress: it not only had the Royal Navy, and huge guns that could destroy any approach from the sea. There were the British and Australian Armies in Malaya next to it.

Margaret and me with Donny Scarlett, and Margaret's friend Helen Webley from next door.

I was now reading easily, and was rarely confused, but for example, I had no idea where or what Corregidor was. I couldn't find it on any map or explanation of it.

There was optimism; we were used to hearing of the successes and the value of the Australians in North Africa and the Middle East. This soon turned to the opposite. The war in Malaya was obviously very different to anything expected. I was surprised to understand that the Japanese rode bicycles along jungle tracks. There was both surprise and shock in all the papers that the Japanese took the Malayan peninsula so quickly. And on Singapore, the island at the tip of the peninsula that was tiny on my maps, there were all the soldiers who had just arrived, and there were all sorts of other people like the doctors and nurses. And the Japanese were going to come in the back way and the guns, "... couldn't be turned around", my mother told me.

Our cousin Thora Berg, holding a koala for Margaret and Me

Very early in the year there was bad news about Uncle Frank. We had heard he was a Petty Officer serving on HMAS Hobart somewhere in the Mediterranean, but we heard he had been taken to hospital from his ship and was in the General Hospital in Alexandria in Egypt. My mother was extremely upset and anxious. I was aware that he was a focus of many of her worries for her younger brother, with both of their parents being dead. I knew intuitively why she was so worried. We learned that it was a kidney. There was discussion about him being in hot engine rooms; he had told us about being able to cook eggs on various metal parts.

Back in Australia. The surgeons at the hospital eventually carried out an operation (Nephrectomy appears on a record) and I understood that he had an abnormal artery to his kidney that was not in the usual place and was blocking the outflow of urine. In the early fifties as a medical student, I was to see a dissection in the anatomy department of such an instance where the renal artery comes off the aorta anomalously and obstructs the ureter.

He will be in the hospital for many weeks, and we know from naval history his ship at that time was the destroyer Napier, that rapidly leaves to fight in the Pacific War.

Soon after, I started school in 4th grade and was just about to turn eight. Miss Liddell was the teacher, and she had a reputation of being very strict. I was cautious with her and quieter in class than I would have been before.

The Religious Instruction teacher was an older Presbyterian minister, who got quickly down to telling us that life was short and that people could die when they were forty and the sinners would go to hell. We as children were going to live the right way or we would almost certainly be there quickly.

I am aware such behaviour to children who are too undeveloped to understand abstract thinking that leaves them highly vulnerable to anxiety and insecurity. As a supervising child psychiatrist, I know it still happens, and usually at private schools where the parents want their child to be separated from secular education.

I was asking about the soldiers going to war. My mother said that some were 'going' when they were seventeen or eighteen. Miss Liddell looked serious: that week was full of: "Who was going to escape from Singapore?" And then, before we had time to be in suspense, the Japanese army had crossed the narrow waterway, and, after some fierce fighting with British and Australian soldiers, were in Singapore and in total control.

The 'grown ups' all seemed to know of various people who were taken prisoner there in early February 1942. The adults changed -- changed from people who counted battle-ships and sent parcels to people in Britain and were proud of our soldiers in North Africa. This was a new war and one that "was in our backyard". As we had read about Europe, the bombs could come here.

On February 18th, I turned eight. The next day the Japanese bombed Darwin. Total surprise, ships were sunk and people killed. The item was: that only two weeks after they take Singapore they are dropping bombs on Darwin. I read everything about it that I could. But I didn't understand the moment of it from what I read. I had heard so much about London and Coventry and Malta that the fact of 'bombing' did not impress me as such.

As an adult I read about the details, and then again in the last twenty years. The overwhelming enormity of it made me understand that it was decided that an already anxious nation did not need to know all the truth that year (I don't think the adults were told any more than I gleaned), but on the other hand it could have come out much earlier. The scale of Japanese force used was of the order of the bombing of Pearl Harbour, although Darwin Harbour did not have the significant targets like Hawaii, but there was extensive loss of life, shipping, planes and infrastructure.

The Scarlett family across the street commenced building an air-raid-shelter in the middle of their backyard — dug deep with sandbags all around. It certainly looked protective.

Because Rabaul had been bombed like this some weeks ago and was soon taken by Japanese forces some days after Darwin was bombed, there was fear that Darwin itself was to be invaded. My mother had said "Rabaul was sort of part of New Guinea but on a big island quite close to it." She said it had lots of volcanoes that would erupt often and there were many earthquakes like New Zealand. But it was a very good harbour for big ships (My mother knew all the places in the world that had earthquakes and volcanos) I found it on the map and was surprised to find that the very big island to the Northwest was called New Britain.

But instead, the Japanese immediately invaded Timor. I could easily find Timor on the map. It made me anxious because looking at the map; Darwin was so far from Melbourne and so close to Timor.

I can remember being very conscious of this when I first visited Darwin just after Cyclone Tracy (Christmas day 1974).

Three places on the North Coast of New Guinea have stuck in my memory: Lae because it was always in the News, and Buna and Gona because my mother spoke about them repeatedly. They were places where the Japanese were held up and where there was repeated fighting with the Australians, mostly I think, when there was a counter-attack later in the war.

She talked often of Timor too, when there were Australians fighting from the mountains and who were being cared for by the Timorese.

A big communal air-raid shelter was to be built on the vacant paddock between Scarlett's lane and Malvern Road.

At school we did something called an 'intelligence test'. Susie, of course was the highest, but I was surprised to come a very clear second, with both of us having big scores.

Now there was much more talk about blackouts and other air-raid precautions and the people selling 'war savings certificates' were pressing everybody again. If you put in sixteen shillings during the war, after the war you would get a pound back. You bought war-savings stamps to put on them. There was also talk about the Americans, because we knew that there had already been some Americans at Darwin.

My mother's roses were maturing and growing marvellously. They would be many long-stemmed blooms, and she would send me off to school almost every week in season with a big bunch freshly picked for Miss Liddell. I could identify them, and I remember one was called President Hoover. I knew he was a president from a long time ago, and that the President of The United States was Franklin Delano Roosevelt. They had talked about him for a long time because of The Depression -- now he was the American Leader alongside Winston Churchill. Mr Churchill only had two names.

Uncle Basil and my father thought the Americans should have been in the war much earlier. My mother said that Mr Curtin was getting the Americans to come to Australia, and he wanted to have Australian troops back from the war against the Nazis to fight the Japanese. I was not aware of Churchill's resistance to this until I was an adult.

At this time there was another loss, this time the HMAS Perth. With an American ship it engaged in a battle with a Japanese fleet but was torpedoed and sunk with the Australian sailors becoming prisoners. This was in the Sunda Straight at our end of Java.

The adults were even more shocked when we woke up one morning to find that Sydney Harbour had been attacked by three Japanese midget submarines. My mother said they were after a big US ship in the Harbour. The news said they had missed the Americans and hit a much smaller ship with their torpedoes. Sailors had been killed. As it was talked about on the wireless, and then by everybody, it did not appear to be a very successful attack, as one submarine had been caught on a net, another had been attacked getting into the Harbour and the third one had used all its torpedoes. A week later two Japanese submarines had been shooting their guns, one at Newcastle and another at Sydney's Eastern suburbs.

The war stories in my English Champion comic/magazine involving the "Spitfire pilots" and 'The Lost Commandos' in Germany were engrossing me and drew my attention back to the war in Europe and its progress more than the adults' conversation. My mother, 'couldn't get any sense out of me' until I had read each one as it arrived.

Then, half way through the year Grade 4 had a major disruption. Miss Liddell was to be leaving and leaving very soon. She was to be married. When women teachers married, they were required to leave their job, my mother explained. Married women could not have jobs that men or unmarried women could do, as it wasn't thought fair for them to have a job that others needed.

I was surprised that Miss Liddell chose me and Geoffrey Evans to help her carry her things home on her last day before her wedding. She had quite a few items in her locker from the staff room. We caught the No7 tram going to Camberwell and went right through Camberwell Junction and over the next hill and then walked with her to her Unit. She gave each of us a chocolate bar that was hard to get and said goodbye to us sadly.

It was around this time, after the old clergyman who taught us religious instruction had been doing the warnings about the disasters after death if we did not do all the Church wanted us to do, that I had sudden and strong intuition that nearly everybody seemed to have these types of belief, with the significant absence of my parents and Aunty Cis — but the common view was not right. My close family was a model of goodness and kindness, didn't seem to think they had to follow all 'the Church stuff'. I was stunned and upset by these intuitive feelings and wanted to question them.

My Sunday-School teacher told me that we knew it was true because all four books of the Bible were telling us the same thing and we must have faith in this. But I was suddenly changed, I was preoccupied by 'cause and effect' in a universal sense, and my anxieties about the supernatural were gone.

There was huge fighting around the Southern Front in Russia, but the Germans still hadn't taken the three main cities. The war in the desert was still going on and The Tirpitz was along the Norwegian Coast and was threatening the convoys going north to Russia. I had been interested in The White Sea when I asked questions in third grade about the Red Sea, the Black Sea and the countries near the North Pole. But it was the Japanese the adults were all talking about.

Soon, General MacArthur arrived in Australia to be the Commander of The War in The Pacific. We saw a lot of photographs of him. His presence in Melbourne where his headquarters were, made people here 'feel better'. I was glad we lived right down the South part of Australia.

The train from Tooronga to Flinder's Street went directly past the Melbourne Cricket Ground, but then, when I would still kneel on the seat to see out the window, my mother told me that was where the American Army Headquarters were, and that they had taken it over now until after the war was over.

By now, those thoughts of all the toys I had before the war, the trips to The Show where I would get all these free samples of food to stock my play grocery store, the various chocolate items, the variety of cheeses, the lights on everywhere (we had started practicing blackouts): these were only triggered when somebody started to talk about such things.

There was a sense of The War going on for a very long time. At these times we would go shopping at Myers or Buckley's, and occasionally we would go to 'the pictures' to see a film usually accompanied by a newsreel about the war.

In May the Japanese Fleet came Southwest from where they had invaded New Britain and The Solomon Islands. The talk at the time was that they would be after Port Moresby the principal city and port of Papua-New Guinea (on its South Coast) and hence have total control over it. At this time Japanese air raids were occurring on the Far North Queensland Coast as well as Darwin. There was a strong feeling that the Japanese were going to do something and there was talk of The Brisbane Line, meaning the Australians were going to defend Brisbane and everything south of it.

I didn't know about this Battle with the Japanese Fleet, or even its likelihood. I didn't hear about it until it was virtually over, and the news (with map) was indicating that the Japanese had sailed into the Coral Sea and that there had been a heavy battle with American and Australian ships taking on the Japanese. We knew it was a strange battle because it was the Aircraft Carriers and their planes that would sink the other side's ships. Fortunately, the planes from the American carriers damaged the Japanese fleet badly. Other planes, both American and Australian were flown into action from the mainland. The important thing was that the Japanese turned back.

While all that happened in The Coral Sea during only four or five days, it was still some days later before the Australian public grasped the importance of what had occurred. It changed most of the worry of Australian families in Melbourne so far away.

Only a month later when the Japanese tried to attack Midway Island the Americans knew they were coming and sank four Aircraft Carriers in an obvious victory.

At this time some 'comics' were being printed. Buck Rogers, Red Rider and Hurricane Hawk would come out monthly (all pictorial with balloon dialogue); Mandrake the Magician and The Phantom would come out in the Women's Weekly and some other magazines. But somehow, we were able to get the weekly Champion from England. It had a well-illustrated paper cover from one of the stories. A reader only 'comic': the regular stories were: Rockfist Rogan the boxing Spitfire pilot, Kangaroo Kennedy an Australian who was a munitions factory worker who was captain of a local football team, Gusty Gale Gets Cracking, a story of the adventures of two fourth form schoolboys at a British boarding school, that I think about every time I hear about Hogwarts. The Leader of the Lost Commandos, who were six men left behind in Germany who lived in the woods and did daring sabotage operations behind German Lines, were immediately evocative of the European war as it happened. Hurry Scurry was an adventurous motor-bike racer who came along later. I read these 'voraciously' and kept them neatly in my bedroom drawer of 'Uncle Frank's wardrobe.'

As a result, reading went from a capable level with books and The Sun and The Herald, to very fast and comprehensive, but was laughable because there were now many familiar words I read that I couldn't say. For example, I said com promise instead of com-prom ise and tew o leen instead of tol yew een. I knew like any child what a promise was, and that T rinitrotoluene was the long name for TNT, one of the most important commodities of The Second World War. I suppose this sort of misunderstanding was inevitable, but I remember serial embarrassment. I can remember thinking that the Gusty Gale characters were in Fourth Form and that I had to wait a long time to be among that age group.

Because the local lending library was run by our family friend Mrs Scott, and she was looking after their three grand-nieces, Shirley, Judy and Leonie, I was able to borrow books easily. I was given a Captain W. E. Johns book, Biggles Flies North and there were more of these to be read, but the library had some shelves of aeroplane stories from the twenties and thirties, not to mention a series of stories about car racing, and I was soon into them.

We children had our own economy in those days when our coins were made of real silver. It was bottles. Soft drink bottles: on each one a deposit had to be paid, and the issuing shops gave a silver threepence for their return. ('threepence' was pronounced abruptly with a silent 'ee') There was always somewhere to scrounge such bottles and various areas where they might be found.

In the newspapers the Japanese were completely taking over the countries to the immediate North of Australia (with the exception of Papua New Guinea where much fighting would continue in the North).

Rommel finally takes Tobruk and again sets out for Cairo. I was aware the Germans were stalemated in the North part of their Russian Front: (I knew what that meant because having thought I'd won a game of chess against my father; he showed me by graphic demonstration of the stalemate for which I had fallen.) But they seemed to be

Margaret and me with Mostly, the dog

winning in The Crimea and I came to know the map of the North Coast of the Black Sea and the peninsula quite well.

There was quite a lot of talk about Rommel that went along the lines that he couldn't possibly keep winning so far from Germany and in the desert too, and there was a theme that he had out-generaled the allies, but they couldn't see him taking Cairo. The adults, (mostly my parents and Uncle Basil) couldn't see Hitler invading England now that the Americans had entered the war. It is interesting that as I am writing this, I can see and hear the old upright wireless cabinet of polished timber going to the blurred music that announced that the news would immediately follow. It became our National Anthem eventually and in contrast can be sung crisply.

At school one of the boys threatened to liquidate another. I later knew it had come from the town of Lidice in Czechoslovakia, where the locals had killed the head of the Nazi SS (Heydrich). It was reported on the news that the Germans had liquidated the whole place - buildings and every person in it.

> It was a word then used by the schoolboys: there were huge differences between boys and girls' behaviour and language in those days, mostly because the playgrounds separated the sexes for some years until a local neologism 'spiflicate' took over from it.

As the jonquils started to bloom in early Spring, another place became talked about -- the Kokoda Trail, or 'The Kokoda Track'. It was, and is, a walking track from Kokoda on the north side of the New Guinea mountains, crossing the Owen Stanley Range to Port Moresby. The Japanese were attempting to get to Port Moresby overland. They were bombing the port anyway. I knew the Australian soldiers were sent to fight them and were heroes in holding them up. As a child I had no idea they were reservists, and that of the two groups one was easily overwhelmed, but the other fought on under terrible conditions for weeks before they were relieved by more Australians.

It was here that my father's conversations with Uncle Basil were helpful. The news was that General MacArthur's forces were holding the Japanese from getting to Port Moresby, when it was all Australians responsible. Australia's General Blamey had more to say about this than he was supposed to.

On the other hand, the American soldiers invaded the Japanese held Solomon Islands and we were aware there was terrible fighting there for many months with many soldiers killed on Guadalcanal. I found the 'canal' very confusing as to what type of war was being fought, whereas I could imagine the Kokoda track with 'The fuzzy-wuzzy angels' carrying the wounded back towards Port Moresby.

Miss Kell arrives to be our new Fourth Grade Teacher. We found her to be a cheerful lady, not easily upset or distracted — 'cheerful' was the word I would have used then. In the last part of fourth grade and in fifth grade I am to receive intensive teaching in grammar. She made this interesting to me, and Susie and Margaret Davis were finding it easy and this spurred me on.

Dictation was a discipline at which I was highly variable, depending on my level of attention (due to various distracting issues I would have running in my head; these were often a dramatic scenario from the characters I had read about, or a war scenario with myself as protagonist. They were often suggestive from the book I was reading at the time.)

At this time the Japanese were not that crippled by the loss of their four aircraft-carriers, because they too sunk some American Carriers and took more Islands in the central Pacific. In the other war, Rommel was pushing East towards Cairo too; the war now occupying the whole world.

At this time my father was often late home and worked longer on Saturdays. He was doing overtime, and this was important to my parents because of the loss of the Tennis Court income and the disintegration of the courts. I listened to their talking, particularly when Uncle Basil came, and we were sitting in the dining area with the very small open fire alight in its grate. I was now responsible for cutting the wood and lighting it. I found out that American submarines and tanks needed all sorts of spare parts that could be made in my father's machine shop. He was teaching and supervising this work.

I knew that the enemy submarines were all over the North Atlantic and that was one of the places where the Germans still seemed to be winning. However, the Japanese submarines we had heard of, were midgets that sneaked up, made their presence felt but didn't do much damage. But we didn't hear about Japanese submarines doing things like the U boats, and I knew the Americans had their own submarines, however we didn't know until after the war about how much damage they did to Japan's lines of supply and naval strength.

While the Kokoda trail fighting was occurring in the high jungle passes of Papua- New Guinea, in the rain, among the mud and leaches, day and night, sometimes hand to hand, we Fourth Grade children were sitting in our school room in Osborne Avenue, and Miss Kell was teaching us grammar and reading us 'Wind in the Willows' of an afternoon. During this eighteen-month period until the end of Fifth Grade, I was accelerating my education, listening to the teachers and highly involved in doing my school work.

At the end of the school year the Japanese retreated from the Kokoda trail, back to the fighting on the North New Guinea Coast where there were Americans and Australians fighting more Japanese troops. I was aware that now the grown-ups were more confident and not afraid of Japanese invasion since Port Moresby survived.

This Christmas, we did not leave home for a holiday, but stayed in Creswick St. My father worked overtime and still worked 6 days a week and we had our own eggs and vegetables. I was to know later that this overtime money was paying off the tennis-courts debt.

Around this time, I was reading everything I could get my hands on, and I would readily get bored and restless if I had nothing to read. I had delved into most of my parents' books by this, but picked up a battered book about a girl called Tess. While the reading of it was easy, the story was awful. What happened to this poor girl was full of blame and helplessness. I felt bad and sick and didn't understand why any of these people would do these things. I didn't talk to my parents about it because I didn't want my reading interfered with. I had bad dreams, a lot of them about the need for protection and about insecurity when you didn't understand what made other people do things to children or each other. I became much less trusting of adults and their changes of face or mood. I was not going to read any more of his books. I still had no idea what the D'Urbervilles were.

It is to be noted that I tried to read Far from the Madding Crowd as an adult and felt strong displeasure and stopped. I was well aware that was not due to the book itself but 'the post-trauma me' still there.

1943

At the end of January 1943, I commenced Fifth Grade. This time there was a new lady teacher, and surprise, her name was Mrs Thompson (Nina). My mother explained to me that they were so short of teachers because all the men had gone to the war, that they had changed their mind and had allowed married women teachers to come back teaching while the war was on. She also said she knew of Mrs Thompson and that everybody said she was a good teacher. That was because she often chatted to particular people up the street shopping (Malvern Rd Tooronga) and she was one of these.

I kept the supply of roses up to Mrs Thompson as I had to Miss Liddell and Miss Kell but didn't think anything special about it except that I was much more skilled at avoiding rose thorns by this time. Mrs Thompson always had a smile for everybody. She even taught me to organise my workbook and try harder with my handwriting, which had alarmed every teacher from the beginning. "People who have good 'handwriting' get the good well-paid jobs when they grow up," they would tell me again. But my writing did improve considerably.

> She taught us a curriculum with grammar being a large part of it: phrases, clauses – subject / object / complement (I can still say 'appear, become, grow, seem and look' and remember why they didn't go with 'an object'). Instead of being bored and withdrawn into my fantasy world of The Lost Commandos (Champion) or being a naval captain, I was into conjunctions and prepositions and how they went into sentences and fitted in various clauses. This supported me in unhappy years of schooling this was always there and stood me well in surviving years of distraction and withdrawal in the classroom. I wonder how much grammar is taught in the Twenty-First Century - particularly in Fifth Grade.

The stability I noticed in the feelings of adults continued. There was still distress about the deaths of soldiers and Mrs Scarlett's eldest son becoming a Prisoner of War of the Japanese in the Dutch East Indies. But there was not the feeling of immediate invasion of Australia by anybody except the Americans.

To a nine-year old boy, the issue was that the American Servicemen had chocolates that were quite unknown since 1939, although I could remember them vaguely, mostly for the hard ones that were very hard to chew for the little bit of chocolate around them. Well, the Lee cousins seemed to acquire enough chocolates to share, and they were extraordinary. There seemed to be an air of excitement about their house and much dressing up and bright red lipstick and new 'hairdos'. I thought the lipstick made them appear repulsive and the behaviour very strange.

I heard snippets from adult other like: "I don't think anything will come of it, we're sure Howard has a wife back in 'the States' — possibly a family too."

As the year opened, I am reading fast and comprehensively. The Melbourne Herald had the most detailed material with frequent maps with arrows and clear marking of Axis and Allied territory.

The push against Rommel is now succeeding daily. Tripoli is captured quickly. This is important because everybody now can sing The United States Marines Anthem and 'The Shores of Tripoli' charged and dramatic, but I know they are not landing from the sea, and that seems a matter of regret.

> This year of writing, 2011, made me feel familiar with Libya: after the first map I saw of The Libyan revolution. I knew its shape, key places, some names were totally new to me like Sirte and Bani Walid, but this Libya was still the Libya where Rommel was retreating towards Tunisia, and early after school started in 1943, Libya is completely cleared.

The Japanese are all North of the Owen Stanley Range in Papua, and there is still fighting in 'The Solomons' where the Americans are in intense battles against large numbers of Japanese dying for their Emperor.

But I am able to think that reading all this information is a way to know deep inside. I still wasn't aware of intuitive knowledge — that things will be alright.

Uncle Frank Hartley (front centre) survived his operation and was back in Australia. He was appointed as an instructor at the engineering school in Melbourne.

About the other side of the world. My mother would still talk about Napoleon's great mistake. Russia was under ice and blizzards, and my mother said the Russians' 'scorched earth policy' would leave the Germans in a terrible position: and I know she is right because the Leningrad and Stalingrad sieges resolve, and Russia is now taking territory back from the Germans – then a whole German Army must surrender.

In Tunisia the German and Italian armies are still trapped and have to surrender. There is talk of 'unconditional surrender'. My parents say that the end of a war can be when both want to stop, but this one will go on until a complete end where the countries will be completely occupied. They are to repeat this to me quite a few times, as if I wouldn't understand it. But I was to hear them talking about it with others, and it being discussed on the news.

Back at the 5th grade Mrs Thompson was sick. There were some temporary teachers, but quite a few days when we had no teacher and were told to sit and read. One of the older girls was the monitor and was told to send anybody who was naughty to Mr Mercovich next door. Dorothy was a quiet girl, and I said something smart to stir her personally. I was sent next door.

Mr Mercovich was a huge man with an enormous head and incessantly chewed tobacco. He always looked angry or irritable and he smelt terrible. He looked very old, but he must have been fit because he walked home and to school every day up a steep hill to Elizabeth St. I know from his date of later retirement that he would have been about 58.

I had to put out my hand and he hit it hard repeatedly with a strap across the palm. I did not say or do anything, I probably just looked frightened.

Donny Monday was a boy who lived immediately opposite the school who had only been with us for some months. He was a quiet gentle boy. He didn't obey one of the monitors, and he went in for his turn. He didn't come back for some time. he'd been crying and he was shaking.

He didn't come back to school the next day and indeed, I never saw him again. The teacher didn't come to school, and it was said they he was sick. Then another child's parents had told her that the Police had been to see the teacher and it was about what he had done to Donny Monday, who had been to the doctor and then the police with his parents. There were numerous stories about what had happened, but they agreed that Donny had severe bruising on his arm, hand and on other parts of his body; and, when the teacher eventually came back to the school the story got around that the Judge or Magistrate among other things had taken his strap away from him, and made it clear that if he physically touched a child he would go to jail and be dismissed.

I remembered thinking that it was fortunate that I hadn't said or done anything to make it worse, and wondered how Donny would have felt when confronted by 'Mucka'. When somebody said 'Mucka' as he was called, they would look around to be sure he wasn't in sight.

My parents were angry, but they could see that something was already being done about the matter. Mrs Thompson came back, and we went on with the calm we were used to.

Lae was the centre of Papua's North coast and the biggest place on the North of Papua-New Guinea. This was the place the Australians and Americans were concentrating on. Japan wanted it, they had tens of thousands of troops controlling large areas of the Solomon Islands to the East' and Dutch East Indies to the West, but they were still on this one bridgehead on New Guinea. There were now bases of American and Australian aircraft there to the East, and, near the top of the Kokoda Trail as I thought about it.

But it was only when the Japanese tried to reinforce Lae with many thousands of soldiers in the one effort that they were vulnerable. They had to cross the substantial Bismarck Sea, and so were hit from the air. More than half of their ships were sunk, although hundreds of troops were rescued from the water and the sinking ships, then taken back to the Japanese base at Rabaul on New Britain.

I am still surprised that many people have little knowledge of The Battle of the Bismarck Sea, the role of the RAAF, or its outcome.

The middle of 1943 was when I gloried in my maps.

The invasion of Sicily took place, and the two areas of territory grew on the map of Sicily. There were many maps of Russia showing where the Germans were being pushed back. Maps were not as good for understanding where the fighting was occurring in the Pacific, but good for understanding where most of the islands and places were. Mostly that was. Guadalcanal confused me totally. I couldn't find it on any map. Nobody had ever heard about it, until it was being talked about all the time and I was a concrete nine-year-old, for all my reading capacity. A canal meant a canal. My mother was steeped in the Suez Canal and its building and had bought the special book that I wish I still had now. The Panama Canal was where thousands of men had died of Yellow Fever when they were building it. But Guadalcanal was a place where there was terrible fighting in very bad conditions where many Americans had already died. We knew it was "a hell hole".

On another day it was decided that I would go to work with my father again and see what he did there. I was still fascinated by all the points and mazes of tracks on the West side of Melbourne. Newport itself was still a dingy place with tiny cottages looking as if they would fall down and had never been painted. I thought the Victorian Railways Workshops huge buildings that had roofs like teeth made of iron. I knew they were there to look after steam locomotives – 'steam engines' as I called them, and knew a lot about how they worked, and already was acquainted with Watt and Stevenson's great discoveries.

Inside, there were the numerous machines each with a man standing at them. I could see the machines cutting though the steel with this 'milky stuff' pouring all over it. I was told it had to be like that to keep it cool and I can still smell it.

This time I was taken to an office where my father talked to the boss of the Workshops (called him Jacko at home) but was aware that my father had to go around all the machines, particularly where younger people were working, and sometimes have to show

Margaret and me with mother's relative, Bert Todhunter on leave from Western Australia.

them how to do something. Sometimes he would measure things; in all, my father said that it was important to see what sort of place he had to work in, and that I was to do well in school so that I could choose a better job. My mother suggested a 'bank manager' like my Uncle Bert (Shepherdson, husband of my father's elder sister Molly) on one of these occasions.

But I was to follow my father into a long room where there was a great line of what looked like small artillery shells on a conveyor belt. I can still see their two colours and that they were shiny. One of the men there in a joking manner questioned whether I had a 'clearance'. I knew straight away that this function was not to be talked about to anybody but tell myself this is okay to add this in October 2013.

My maps suggested to me we are winning the war.

I was getting very good marks for my schoolwork and was also keeping up with Susie and Margaret Davis. Then one morning my mother woke me up for school, (my father left for work at just after 6 am) and told me that the Germans had been totally surprised because the Allies had bombed the dams in the Ruhr. They'd broken the dams and huge floods had gone into the Germans' factories. The dams were used for electricity to run their factories. She said that nobody had thought they could do this to the dams.

Margaret and me on my birthday, February 1943.

I learnt more, as it was told again and again, and I imagined the Germans guns shooting at the planes as they were coming in very low over the water. But then my mother found that a distant cousin of hers was part of the raid and she would tell the story in more detail and more often. I even understood that her Granny Skead (nee Lewis) was Keith Astbury's Grandfather's much older sister. (The papers called him Colin, but he was known in the family by his middle name). My mother's great, great grandparents, Daniel and Elizabeth Astbury, had been the migrants who came out with their children from Staffordshire in the eighteen forties, very soon after Melbourne was founded in 1834, where they first lived in a tent. The story as told by my mother was noted by the fact that they had a Tavern in early Melbourne town that was still there, just off Collins St in the heart of Melbourne, and what a pity it didn't stay in the family.

> *The Mitre Tavern is Melbourne's oldest building, and now has a photo of Elizabeth Astbury, presented to it by our cousin Charlie Lewis. Later we were to find the records of Granny Skead's birth in the upstairs room of the Mitre Tavern to Elizabeth Astbury's eldest daughter, also Elizabeth, who was married to Henry William Lewis. And her mother Elisabeth Astbury was the midwife — all three Elizabeth. Note: See photographs at end of chapter.*

Next door in Creswick St, young Kevin Doyle started to keep rabbits and later pigeons. We were able to get a pair of domestic rabbits and my father made a rabbit hutch of timber and iron with a hinged front door with tennis wire to see through. This was to be a source of great wonder, and then source of tragedy as the male rabbit trampled the baby rabbits to death immediately after they were born. A larger, two compartmented hutch was made and this time the babies were safe and growing. Much later dogs raided the back yard in the middle of the night and killed them all. My distress about this lasted many months.

At this stage I was consoled by flavoured milkshakes and lemonade sold by 'Chelle', Mrs Michelle, as we called her, at the milk bar close by. My bottle finding economy was consistent.

My father was working later at night and on a Saturday. I knew my parents had lost their worries about money they had earlier in the war and remembered a time when my mother had cleaned out my money box one week to 'buy things up the street' but she had given it back to me the following week. "Dad's overtime is paying off the tennis court debt", my mother told me, but then new insecurity arose. My now four-year-old sister and I had found that we could throw pillows and then cushions at each other with great glee. I threw one that hit the large white glass light fitting in the middle of the lounge room. Crash! it fell down and broke to numerous small pieces. Our mother was distraught. "We don't own the house and the fittings like this, they belong to Uncle Joe." (Joseph Justins)

My parents advised me that when they were buying the tennis courts, they needed to have a house that connected with them, and they couldn't buy both. Uncle Joe had come in and bought the house (Neither he nor his two brothers were married or had children.) and we were saving up to buy it from him when we could. Uncle Joe was a fixture in that he usually came of a Sunday morning on the train, and he would sit around chatting about events to do with the war, and the various relations and friends and would leave when he was ready. He was in his late seventies even then. They weren't interesting conversations, such as my father and his brother Basil talking intensely about the war but were more background like my mother talking to her friends on the telephone.

The old phone number flashes into my mind as I write. I would always answer 'Tooronga Tennis Courts'.

So, I wasn't surprised about the events that followed a storm, during which it rained hard and the house's high gable on the bedroom side that only had my window in it, got very wet, and the cement charcoal render sagged, and then mostly fell off all over this wall, leaving the wooden lathes bare. There was a lot of looking at it with Uncle Joe and workmen. They pulled it all off and then put weatherboards across it. The weather boards were evidently very hard to come by as new building of any kind other than for the military was stopped. Eventually it was all painted and finished.

This was a time of Uniforms. I liked Joe Scarlett's navy uniform best. The schoolboy down the road, Pearce Morgan now had a blue Air-force Uniform as had Cousin Ivan from Swan Hill/Ultimo an older brother of Win, Myra and Marion Young who had stayed with us various times as they were getting live-in housemaid jobs at some of the nearby big houses.

The American uniforms always looked smart and seemed to have better colours with goldy brown tones to them. My map fascination is given a big boost when the Brits and then the Americans land in Italy. The Italians surrender quickly but it doesn't mean anything because the German Armies there: take over Rome, and Mussolini is still with them and it all has to be fought over bit by bit and the map advances accordingly.

The Americans have to take Islands in the Pacific one by one, and for them it is a bitter war as so many soldiers are to be killed to take each Island. My mother says that coral makes very good airstrips and that the Americans can build them quickly to put aeroplanes on them. I know there is still fighting on Bougainville, the very big Island to the east of Papua New Guinea.

We are coming up to Christmas that year and our cousin Ivan is transferred to the Heidelberg Military hospital in northeastern Melbourne because he has 'a nasty infection in his ear'. My mother thinks he will be alright because the new 'sulphur drugs' are available for serious infections, but I can tell the adults are worried about this. Then in a few days I hear it is in his 'mastoid'. The doctors have to operate. My mother says that the mastoid is a bony place that is near the brain. Aunty Midge is very upset and even Aunty Nell is distracted from her own goings on. There are many phone calls about it. I hear the word 'mastoid' many times and then meningitis. My mother is hugely distressed, anticipating that he will die now. And she was right. He died in the next couple of days. The relatives from Swan Hill arrived quickly and many others gathered from nearby for the funeral.

Aunty Midge's home at 10 Creswick St, became the centre of this gathering. Aunty Myra, Ivan's mother, seemed to continually cry and Aunty Midge with her. Crying people, I wasn't sure who they were, grabbed me and hugged me.

I can remember them all climbing into big cars to go to the funeral still crying. I didn't think about why my mother had done all her crying just before he died and why she stayed home from the funeral.

> I can remember ten or twelve years later as a medical student thinking, "Aha, that is what happened to Ivan, and then that... " — knowing then that medicine of the 1950's had advanced so much Ivan would have had a strong chance of being saved. I'm sure it made me treat every case of Otitis-Media in General Practice seriously and cautiously, and I felt angry at a mother who had waited until her daughter had a high fever, pus was pouring from the ear and there was bony tenderness before she sought medical attention. I contained my anger and being aware of Ivan in the background as the cause of it. This child in the early sixties of course did very well in the short term, but I did not see the eventual damage to the eardrum.

Bessie Skead nee Lewis, granddaughter of Elizabeth Astbury nee Tharme. Kate Hartley nee Skead, daughter of Bessie. Frank in the middle and Freda standing. Freda and Frank with mother and grandmother.

Elizabeth Astbury nee Tharme. Arrived in Victoria, 1849. The family hosted The Mitre Tavern where Bessie Skead was born, 1854.

1944

This was a time when the war did not seem dangerous — only long. My mother would dwell on what the German people might be suffering now that it was German cities being bombed heavily. There were many pictures of the Lancasters, and I knew they kept making more and more of them, and that the Americans were in England with their own aircraft adding to this. I knew the Germans had fighter planes that shot down a large number of the bombers.

I was also aware that the large city of Hamburg had been almost totally destroyed by a huge bombing raid that had set it on fire as well as blowing it up. But the adults around me were not threatened by the war in Europe unless they had somebody fighting there, and then it was mostly those taken prisoner by the Japanese and those fighting in the Pacific that distressed them specifically.

Writing now on Easter Sunday 2012, I can tell you that my long periods of not writing this account, are not my outward excuse to Margaret about working very hard and always having work material hanging over my head — true, but I was blocked because 1944 was a distressing painful year for me, and one I never forget during my teaching of young psychiatrists to become Consultant Child and Adolescent Psychiatrists. Indeed, when I become aware of abuse to children in a classroom, particularly multiple children, I am at the Education Administrators' offices delineating complaints about teacher and principal. This happened rarely because I found there had to be failure at both levels at the school for it to occur.

It was my year to be 'taught' by 'Mucka' — Mr Mercovich, and the origins of my educational failure over the following five years.

Despite my knowing his strap had been taken from him by The Court, I was still very anxious. I listened to everything he said about anything those first weeks. On the second day he set us an examination of our fifth-grade work. I always had a good memory, and can still remember Mrs Thomson's teaching of grammar to this day — and to think she was unable to work in her earlier married years, and was only there teaching because of the war, seems bizarre.

I did the exam carefully as I would have done it for her. While at some level it was a triumph it was a terrible mistake. Having never outdone Susie at anything, I had the maximum marks on my own. Mr Orams the Principal wanted to see me, and Mucka went with me. Mr Orams was quite taken with what I had done and was warm and enthusiastic about what I had achieved — I did not appreciate that some of this may have been because I was still nine. But I was noticed: I stood out for Mucka.

I only realised later as an adult that they would view my ability correctly as a product of Mrs Thompson's teaching. How would his massive ego deal with that, particularly for a child who was almost paralysed by fear of him?

I didn't answer questions and didn't ask questions. I would find him watching me at times. I would avoid returning his gaze. I put much effort into my avoidance. The worse time was when he came around to inspect our workbooks; that's when I would tremble. It was the smell, very close it was a breath smell, different from the body smell. On one occasion, he leant over me. "Rubbish." he exclaimed, doing a twisting movement that knocked by workbook to the floor and then turned away. When I picked it up it had a large brown stain on where he had dribbled his tobacco juice. I eventually showed my parents some weeks after the incident occurred. I was having difficulty going to school on many mornings.

I would be 'sick in the stomach", I would get very distressed when my mother pushed me to go to school, and I knew she would not accept it the second day.

I overheard her telling one of her friends on the telephone that ," ...was not happy at school this year."

My parents decided to put me in the Boy Scouts, and I went along to the 14th Malvern troop once a week. My father helped me with my knots and various other tasks I needed to complete before I would get my uniform. Some of the older boys from my class joined too, one of whom had bullied me for years by putting me to the ground with an arm and foot tackle almost every time he encountered me. However, these Scouts were fairly heavily supervised and task oriented. Essentially, they were an Anglican Church group with a well-meaning view of the Scout movement. 'Scouts' was a lift to my fairly limited life at this time.

The school doctors came around that year to examine all the children. I had my examination, but after that was over, Mr Mercovich had me sent back to the doctor to be examined again. I can only guess why. The doctor repeated some of the things he had previously done and sent me back again. My parents were not aware of what this was about.

I did not stop reading newspapers at all; rather I became obsessed with every war movement. It was now like watching a football match where your side is steadily winning, but it is only just past half time. My mother's 'Napoleon's mistake' theory of the war in Russia is being totally validated, but the Germans fight hard for every part of Northern Italy.

In the Pacific I know New Guinea, and Rabaul on New Britain, but when the Americans are taking the war to the Japanese in the various Islands which have place names on them, the strategic importance of each was beyond my reach. Europe is 'land', and the state of play there is much clearer to me. But the Pacific is aircraft carriers, landing fields, fuel and the need to fight both enemy planes and ships, and the range of where the aircraft can travel: this is a new type of war.

If there is a land battle, as in New Guinea the Japanese are brave and persistent fighters, with concrete bunkers and 'pill boxes' and are very hard to dislodge, so that type of local warfare was understood. But you would have to look up anything with the name 'Island' after it, but then they didn't say 'Island' after some of the places like Okinawa and Iwo Jima. As a rapid reader, I thought it was Two Jima because I'd only read it, and later when I heard of 'Ee wah Jeema' it didn't click with Two Jyma. And then I didn't know Guam and the Marianas were the same, and particularly that it was in the south of the chain and also the largest. Perhaps my difficulty was another issue: when I talked about any place in Europe or the U.K., my parents would know something about it, but they were having to learn new things themselves about the Pacific.

Back in the 6th grade classroom I'd found that the sixth grade had its own little reading library, and Margaret Davis who was one day to be a fellow medical student was the librarian. There were many stories about animals that were very easy reading for me, some simplified classics and some original Australian.

I borrowed them regularly and often had a new one the next day.

This may seem strange behaviour, but in 1944 television was not to arrive before I graduated in Medicine in 1956.

During the year, Mr Mercovich asked before the class who was reading from the Library and how much? Miss Davis replied that it was me, but said, "He doesn't really read them," in a 'voice'.

I was afraid of attention, but her comment made the whole issue die and that was a relief. By then it was no issue for me, because I'd read all I wanted to read of them by then.

I still lay low: I broke no rules. I didn't talk. After some months I would run fictional scenarios in my head that gained more and more details. They were a mixture of WW II pilot or submarine stories, or Wild West with Serial themes from The Pictures such as the Cisco Kid. I also did little cartoons, single strip comic scenarios (in my imagination) of Mucka as the unfortunate victim of humorous calamities. Looking back, I think this was a sign that I was less depressed and functioning better. If I got up early, my mother would hit the tennis balls back for me before I went to school. This was on the one playable tennis court that a women's group would use once a week. The Brightly Painted Tennis Pavilion of the thirties was going to dirt, cracked paint and spiders, as nobody went into it anymore.

The fighting in Italy was very intense, and I remember two places particularly where it

Margaret on her first day at school.

went on for month after month.

The first one was Anzio, the Allies' landing place on the West Coast, and it is in my mind because it was repeated in the news, and it always made me think of ANZAC and 'anz everything else,' Hitler had all his armies there and he had demanded that they were to fight hard and not be defeated. The Allies had landed there instead of coming all the way up the calf of the Italian leg.

My father said there were all sorts of soldiers from many different countries fighting there. I can remember asking him why the people of any country where the Nazis were, didn't start fighting them. That's when he told me they would then take a group of any local people and shoot them all. It explained why they were shooting townspeople in a film I'd seen some years earlier. But I also knew of Resistance fighters in France and Chetniks in Yugoslavia.

The Monte Cassino monastery was a huge building on the top of a high rocky plateau. The fortifications on the mountain were well prepared. It was shown on the newsreels at 'The Pictures', and sometimes we went into a little Newsreel theatre in Swanston St where it was running all the time, and you left when they were repeating the bit you had already seen. overlooking a town. This was not a time when the army rolled on and the map lines moved every day. Hitler's forces were counter attacking and many Allies were killed, and their guns and tanks destroyed.

Easter passed and still this was continuing, until the Germans lost some ground here and were pushed back there, and then there was a very big push that led to the taking of Monte Cassino. Rome was not far away, and the enemy started to fall back.

In Russia there was fighting in the South around the Crimea and towards the city of Odessa on the Black Sea. I knew the Russians were going to keep winning, but they wanted the war to be going on in Europe itself to take the pressure away from them. Instead, there were convoys of ships sailing north from Britain to go all the way around the North of Norway to a Russian port called Murmansk. This was my White Sea again.

This journey was very dangerous as German submarines were waiting for these convoys and many ships were sunk. I can remember a newspaper doing a big spread setting out how U boats would go into special underground pens on the Axis coasts that made them very hard to attack when they were in port. Somebody said it was one part of the war the Nazis were still winning.

But thinking of what I knew that year, it was patchy; and what was happening was so much to keep track of, yet I realise I was withdrawn and miserable and putting my energy into self-protective tactics avoiding being noticed.

The curriculum was much more extensive than any earlier class. I paid enough attention to understand decimals and percentages. There were extensive pieces of history, a major part of which was about The Prophet's rise to power and the beginnings of Islam. Mercovich's view of this was the times and dates, plus disrespect and attempts at humour. I knew from my mother that the Arabs had kept all the learning through The Dark Ages, including the numbers we use today, especially the nought that put me into first grade early, as well as my father's respect for Omar Khayyam: these were quite contrary opinions.

Perhaps this even influenced my later interest in Sufism.

Earlier in the year Merkovich had given us a long spiel about how Catholics like himself were a persecuted minority, and that going to Law was a terrible thing to do because the lawyers were all there for themselves and could twist anything people said. That description did not apply to my Catholic relatives, particularly my grandfather who had been a Collins / Queens St barrister. As a child I did not realise that Mercovich may have been sued in a civil Court as well as going before the magistrate for assault. Nor did I realise that my laying low (in Brer Fox's sense) was an effective defence for these reasons alone. I was very brittle that year and any front-

on confrontation' with or without violence, would have broken me up completely.

Then in the first week of June, an American Army enters Rome. Hitler had ordered his armies to retreat the day before.

To me it was a big day because it had taken month after month and it had seemed so slow, and it was so necessary. President Roosevelt addresses the world to tell how symbolic for the world Rome falling is. But before we can even think about this – D Day really comes the very next day. Like the fall of Rome, it took a very long time, but now it is everything.

I am suddenly alert and want to know the whole pattern of it. After school, my mother said they had invaded France on the Cherbourg Peninsula. I had never heard of this part of France. My father got home from work about an hour and a half later. He was wanting to know what was happening too. We kept the wireless on and if they stopped saying things, I would turn from 3DB to 3LO or another station to pick up more. I quickly understood that thousands had parachuted inland, but I was astounded about the gliders. I had no idea that they could get so many troops in that way. They had tried very hard to keep it a secret, because I knew quite a bit about Anzac Cove and how they had to come up the beaches while being shot by machine guns and artillery. And that was happening too, particularly the Americans at the beach called Omaha. Hundreds were killed in the first half hour. I can remember thinking that the paratroopers were there to stop the Germans sending thousands of troops and guns to attack them before they could get themselves together.

Stuck in my memory were 'the Cherbourg Peninsula', the gliders, and later the 'Whales' that were part of a prefabricated harbour when put together with a pontoon, but big enough for trucks and tanks, but that didn't happen until the next week.

I had a new lot of maps to follow.

The other prominent issues at that time were the V1 pilotless planes dropping on London. Their engine would stop, and they would fall and explode killing numerous people close by, but even people within half a mile could be killed by flying glass or bits of brick. The papers described that the people would hear this loud engine noise coming closer and closer, and it would then stop, while the 'doodle bug', as they called it, dropped from the sky, often onto a highly populated area. The silent period between the engine noise and the explosion was a penetrating terror.

These started early in June, and it wasn't long before the Londoners knew they were under attack again. Defences against them were possible, they could be shot down, and there were precautions that could be taken against flying glass and debris. The armies in France and the RAF could put high priority to dealing with their launch sites, but the anti-aircraft defences of London had to be stopped because the doodlebug would still fall and explode. Such guns were taken to the coast. After these V1 attacks had been going for some months, I saw a depiction showing how a fighter plane could fly parallel to one and position its wingtip under the doodle-bug's air intake, almost touching it and the flying bomb would drop out of the sky as its engine failed.

" Doodlebugs "

LONDON, June 19.— It has .been disclosed that one of the favourite current sports of fighter-bomber pilots is shooting Hitler's pilotless planes. or "Doodlebugs," as the Americans call them. Mustang and Thunderbolt pilots each destroyed some.

Said one Mustang pilot : . "Doodlbug hunting is a lot of fun'— they can't shoot back."

APA citation

"Doodlebugs" (1944, June 21). Daily Mercury (Mackay, Qld. : 1906 - 1954), p. 1. Retrieved April 4, 2024, from http://nla.gov.au/nla.news-article170851870

Nevertheless, thousands of Londoners were killed by these, but by early September with their launch sites compromised, or taken by allied soldiers or destroyed by RAF attacks, they slowed to a stop. But, within days a huge explosion without warning occurred in the London outskirts. It was the first of the V2 strikes. The V2 was a rocket missile weighing tons that came at faster than the speed of sound and travelled from further away. Fortunately, they came singly and sporadically, unlike the V1 s that had been coming up to 100 a day. Reading about these in the Melbourne Herald, it made me anxious to see what the future of warfare might be like if such launch vehicles were used.

While the V2 was an effective terror weapon, it was not doing any harm to the allied war effort, rather it was pushing it to greater effort. In contrast to today's missiles, the V2 guidance system could not take them to any target; they were simply pointed in the right direction and range and let go to hit what they would. I knew that one of them hit a church full of worshippers, killing over a hundred people.

During the months while the V1s and V2s were used on Southern England, the Germans did an all-out attack on the advancing allied armies in France, by coming down at them from the North. There were huge episodes of battle and the Americans had to hold ground they had already won. To me, it was big arrows on the war maps in the Melbourne Herald, pointing at the area already won by the advance.

Despite the rockets, or this counterattack later called The Battle of the Bulge, the grown-ups weren't in the slightest concerned that it could alter what was now an inevitable winding up of The War in Europe. Despite this they were aware that an enormous amount of fighting to the last man would occur with the Japanese: even after taking the major Islands close to Japan, they would then have to take Japan itself. These were my confusing nemeses: Iwo Jima and Okinawa. As 1944 draws to a close, they are able to bomb Eewah Jeema.

After the fall of Rome Uncle Basil was more preoccupied about the Pope, what he had done and particularly what he hadn't done. That subject my father would never bring up, and about which my mother had no interest. But Uncle Basil had a lot to say about it, and particularly about the Pope's infallibility. This word I did not understand, and, even when it was explained to me, I did not know why it was so important or what it really meant about the Pope - it was a word without meaning that obviously had meaning to the adults. Was the Pope a collaborator? Will he take responsibility? This I understood because the notion about Quisling had been explained to me fully as an example of how new words can come into the language. That was my mother. Looking back on it, I am sure that Uncle Basil had great concerns about The Pope and what he could have done, but he couldn't air them to anybody but my father.

I was more aware of the closeness of these two brothers than most, because they let me stay and listen to their conversations   Reg was still in primary school when his father Fred Rickarby died in 1914.

Basil was about 6 years older. My father was bitter about the beatings he had taken during his school and altar-boy years. He became a mason. Basil hadn't rocked the boat, and stayed in the Catholic System, yet was its most detailed critic, but couldn't show that part of him in his own family or circle.

Fred's early death meant his widow Isabella nee Young was left unable to support her four children, but her brothers came to her rescue and set up the boarding house that was tenable for her to care for the four children.

The Young brothers were Presbyterian, and their sisters were Catholic, an aspect of an agreement my great-grandparents Scottish Tom Young and Irish Bridget McCarthy made at the time they married. (Their descendants therefore occupy different sections of the Yarra Glen cemetery.)

There is a book developed from my great-grandfather Thomas Young's diary, called The Golden days of the Caledonian Diggings by Mick Woiwod.

The newspapers I was reading, sounded very doubtful about The Pope too. I understood what Mr Chamberlain had done or didn't do, and why he has remained so criticised; it sounded something like that.

As I was writing about 1944, I became conscious about my greater perception about what had been happening at many levels, and how that had not only altered what I was able to write, but aware that it had developed gradually, making the content easier, but the nuances more complex.

Some issues did come through my preoccupations. I was still following The Allies progress on the maps of Europe, and later when it came to Paris, my mother was talking about how the Germans were to have destroyed Paris, but at the last minute, had escaped without doing this. This was very important to her.

Class photo 1944, I am on the far right.

From the school photo 1944.

1945

Gardiner Central School

*Childhood is a long long time
and each, we've had our own;
seeming, drawn along the line,
along the many lines of self –
slowly, days so long:*

QB Willowby AKA GA Rickarby

SCOUTS
1944 — 1945

I attend my first Scout Camp at Gilwell, not far from the town of Gembrook: east of Melbourne, rough wooded country with many small streams (the Dandenong Ranges). There was much discomfort and eating strange foods, particularly Camp-pie, a tinned version of Beef and Mutton offal in a jelly. Here is a ten-year old who piled more blanket on top of himself rather than insulating himself from the cold groundsheet beneath, and wishing he had blanket pins like most of other boys. It was totally cut off from the outside world, except for meeting other Scout Troops at the major swimming-hole.

Not a word from the family or the war, just learning to survive on an unfamiliar repulsive diet. No milkshakes at Mrs Michelle's, no pancakes or sweet lamb chops from my mother. I was very appreciative of home when I returned, but I did not go on another Scout Camp until I'd joined a different troop about three years later.

The family did not go on holidays that year because we were entering a big New Year where the parents thought the war's circumstances would really improve, but they couldn't yet see its end.

Me (circled) in the Class photo 1945

The war - Japan.

Nineteen-forty-five started quietly – midwinter in the Northern Hemisphere perhaps, so it was not surprising the activity was in Burma and then the Philippines. In Burma we knew the Japanese were fighting back hard, and another seemingly strange new issue entered the Pacific War.

U.S. ships going to the Northern Philippines were highly protected yet were set upon by Japanese pilots flying low into 'withering fire' to crash their plane into American ships and aircraft carriers. Many were shot into the sea and never reached their target. They landed with huge damage to the ship, particularly by setting fire with aviation fuel. Each pilot would give his life to set back the Allied advances in even a small way.

We heard the phrase Suicide Bombers, but 'kamikaze' was taken up by everybody, as if it was necessary to explain something unthinkable for Western society. We children, used to the great risks Allied pilots took, were baffled by this as it seemed unthinkable. I thought of it as a sort of madness because they were losing the war.

In Europe

Very early in 1945 my mother told me the Russians had found German concentration camps where they killed Jews and put people to work as slaves. I remembered the news-reels about how the Nazis would go around Germany writing things on Jewish shop fronts and bashing and arresting them before the war even started. But the unthinkable horror of what they had been doing to the Jews was still unimaginable at this stage of the War.

Year 7 at Gardiner Central

In early December 1944 we did an examination for the High-School part of Gardiner Central (upstairs). 'Central' meant that five other primary schools from the North and the East of us would be sorted into six classrooms over Year 7 and Year 8. Year 7 started again as Form 1 — the possibilities were Form 1A, Form 1B, and Form 1C. I always enjoyed doing exams and did this one (Arithmetic, English and IQ) with the added benefits of being stimulated and away from the Grade 6 classroom. I didn't expect much of myself but was astounded to come seventh.

For once we knew nothing of the potential teachers, except for a neat little middle-aged man called Mr Brown who often did playground duty.

In the last days of January, we turned up to the school, and ascended the stairs (stairs we were not allowed on during primary school days, except for the rare occasion we were allowed to the third-floor area to watch a film.)

We quickly found which form we were in. To my pleasant surprise the 1A class was allotted the Science Room, It had its own little office for the science teacher and science items. Not only that, but the teacher who promptly arrived, was a young woman with neat long blond hair contained in a sort of light net you could hardly see. By anybody's standards she was extraordinarily beautiful. Her name was Miss Shirley Lindner and she taught only science and maths, and for us she started the day for roll call. We learnt from one of the other teachers that she was "brilliant", and via another child's parent, that she was engaged to an American Officer. The other issue was that the majority of the class were strangers. Miss Lindner got us each to say which school we had come from and say our names.

For science, she demonstrated everything with an experiment. I remember the graphic effect of the kerosene can collapsing as she put the vacuum pump on it, and the floating candle that went out gradually after she upended a gas jar over it, and how the water would then rise about a fifth of the way, and how lime water would turn milky when testing for carbon dioxide.

I listened to everything in the science lessons but had no idea how much she would help me when the world moved abruptly into a new age exactly six months later.

I was very bound up in my thoughts about science, nature, the implausibility of the religious beliefs of all adults, and a bewilderment about what this all meant, let alone the way, how and when the war might end. I knew it would end in Europe as the Allies coming into Germany from the South and West and the Russians hurrying to crush them from the other direction. But each Island that was the centre of the Pacific war, seemed to go on for so long and hard with such loss of life, that it would be going for an uncertain time.

In my year up to now, whilst I was aware that I had not been able to keep up with sporting things, I was somehow, included such as keeping cricket scores and looking after things, but having a different sort of life. Mostly in my head I would say….

At the same stage the teachers must have got together and organised a cricket match between upstairs 7 and 8, and downstairs 5 and 6, and surprisingly I got to be captain of the 7 and 8. Years 7 and 8 came from all different primary schools, they came to school by bus, car and dad's motor bike, quite different from us locals who walked.

My background of years of street cricket in Creswick St must have contributed. I was wicket keeper and batsman number 2, — caught out for 12, but hitting well at the Cricket Field in Carroll Crescent (Gardiner Park).

The problem too was that I was now so used to quietly 'tuning out' that, with the exception of science, I lived in my own internal world as I had done in adapting to Mucca in the previous year. I wasn't listening even when Miss Lindner talked about 'x' the unknown number. On the other hand, I was reading extensively, and keeping up with everything in the newspapers about the war.

> Passive, poor, inept, depressed;
> and yet were joys there unexpressed
> when the young and tolerant year
> skimmed along on trains and trams
> and day dreams nearly real held sway
>
> *QB Willowby AKA GA Rickarby*

The war in Europe

While the Germans had been sending over V2s, for the Allies, special bombs were being made for the Dambusters and in the sinking of the Tirpitz. We heard early about very big bombs called Blockbusters, but now the Allies had huge bombs, my mother said thousands of pounds, to drop on special targets. The big Krupp factories in the Ruhr that had never stopped until this time, were finally bombed to a standstill.

Then came the bombing of a beautiful city that had hardly been touched: Dresden, said to be a railway junction for the German war effort against the rapidly advancing Russians. My mother said she thought there was some agreement with the Germans to mutually avoid destroying buildings of high significance. But it turned into a poorly selected bombing, a huge bombing — and a fire-bombing. There were many people killed, including many refugees.

Japan

The USA had taken Islands close enough to Japan to be able to bomb Japan itself.. The Americans used incendiaries. We heard that Japanese cities burned easily but could not imagine what it would be like for the recipients. We were told they really meant to fight to the last soldiers alive and had guns for everybody. They did this on every Island taken in the Pacific.

The two big steps to Japan were Iwo Jima and Okinawa. Newsreels reports Kamikaze attacks on all Allied shipping near Okinawa were intense, persistent, and aimed at causing serious damage. Okinawa would be close enough for air attacks from Mainland Japan.

To the South, the Americans were systematically retaking the Philippines, while Manila was taken back during March. (I still didn't know where Corregidor was.)

The newsreels showed short clips of planes diving towards the camera, and the gun emplacement on the ship's manoeuvrable automatic weapon rapid-firing tracer directly at them. Some war artists created remarkable coloured pictures of the sea wars between carriers and incoming planes – a sense of all this khaki, flame, smoke, against the deep blue ocean, dotted with white plumes and shell bursts.

I was growing up in some ways. Now I was in High School, even if it was on top of my previous primary school, mostly directly above the room I'd started in before the war - Kindergarten class. But I was now aware that the war was happening quickly compared to the earlier stages. It wasn't just me thinking my life was going faster, it was also true.

I was reading many newspapers and other materials. I had the wireless on to the short-wave news. I was also seeing many more newsreels, taking myself to 'the flicks.'

I had isolated myself in my inner withdrawn world during my defended year with Mr Mercovich. I still did this, absorbed in scenarios of my imagination.

Science

I lifted out of this withdrawal for Miss Lindner's science lessons, but not for the beginnings of algebra and geometry. I remembered Mrs Dogood, mostly for her extreme dislike of being addressed as 'Miss'. " I am a Mrs - Mrs Dogood!", she would say emphatically, interrupting whatever else was happening. She had come back to teaching as a married woman to be an English teacher at High School level. She kept the classroom warm and alive.

More war

But each island of the Pacific war – long and hard with some loss of life – and it is going for an uncertain time.

The maps in the newspapers were moving quickly on all three fronts. In Europe, big cities like Paris, and in the Philippines, Manila was free, and while the Germans were still fighting in Northern France, every front was closing on them. In Yugoslavia and southern France, the Resistance was coming out and openly fighting the enemy — Partisans they were called. There were wonderful spy stories about special agents being dropped in France to help the Resistance, and help shot-down pilots to escape to Spain.

These changes were all very different to the long drawn out fighting against the Afrika

Corps, and the slow bit in Italy before Rome fell. In early March the newspapers were focusing on the Rhine, and it stood out on all the maps. There were concerns expressed that the Germans might stop the Allies at crossing points, because they were destroying all the bridges.

It was certainly a brave and determined American Unit to fight their way to the other end and secure it, making a huge difference to the advance of the British and American armies. My parents talked about how enraged Hitler would be because the Axis propaganda was that they would hold the East Bank of the Rhine.

Iwo Jima

On Iwo Jima many thousands of Japanese were dug in to defend it. The newsreel man with the high-pitched excited voice said it was this island that must be taken for airfields to attack Japan and other Pacific islands. This included the big one, the next one – Okinawa.

They said that that every Japanese soldier would fight until he was killed. Unlike a lot of the other news of the time that seemed to happen in a single day, Iwo Jima took a month and left the legacy of 'the flag raising photograph' as a reminder of one of the most important campaigns and most expensive of lives of the Pacific War.

The fighting for Iwo Jima was really over in the middle of March.

I did not know about the retaking of Corregidor. I still had no idea where it was. It was taken about a month before Iwo Jima.

The war news.

The war news was full of details. I knew every position in a Lancaster bomber as I had known of the Blenheim bomber earlier in the war. I knew there were now hundreds, and they were being shot down often, and that the crews had a big chance of dying every time they went out. They were bombing big cities and bombing ahead of the army advances, and that these airmen were part of the now inevitable defeat of Nazi Germany.

In the Pacific war I immediately noticed the Allies taking Mandalay in Burma. I knew the 'Road to Mandalay' song even to the second verse, and I knew just where it was, in contrast to my confusion about the Pacific War place names, and my clarity about European place names.

Personal recovery

At school I had escaped from Mucka to a very relaxed atmosphere and was surrounded by a decent lot of children being taught by kind teachers, yet I dreamed my way throughout, in what I now know was the beginning of a personal recovery from 1944. I sat up and took in every item of science but drifted through the others with my self-entertaining imagination. This may have been the time that the school photo was taken with me smiling, holding the class board, centre front.

Yet Miss Lindner woke me up with very detailed lessons about the solar system and our own place in it. Reading Buck Rogers since I was about six or seven, I was familiar with the idea, but now the reality seemed to be more wonderful.

Despite my usual withdrawal during school — at home I was reading avidly — the newspapers were still being absorbed in detail.

Europe

My father and Uncle Basil were now talking about the Russians: how strong their army was and how ruthlessly they were destroying the Germans on their westward push into Germany itself. We heard that the soldiers from the Eastern parts of the Soviet Union were like wild men, killing and looting and that both the Allies and the Russians were racing to get to Berlin first and that Churchill was very worried by this. The papers said that the Allies had stopped at the Elbe River.

Then within days everybody knew the Russians were certainly getting to Berlin first.

This was the week in April when President Roosevelt dies of a stroke very suddenly. Everybody is shocked. He was the American President everybody loved and respected.

But this week was followed by unbelievable horror. The British Army came upon the Belsen Concentration Camp near Hanover. The Melbourne papers published graphic photographs of walking skeletons, massed corpses, all starvation riven, on the brink of death from camp plagues and infestations on top of their foodless state. My mother was in a state of shock that humans could be like this: she kept coming back to tell me about the awful things the Nazis did to a wide range of people as well as their total persecution of the Jews.

I saw newspaper photos, one of which is still imprinted, of what I at first saw as a man walking on the bones of his legs like sticks, and the eyes sticking out from a fleshless face — all eyes, looking upward to the camera with mouth half open, and then I realised it was a woman from the hairless face.

President Truman did not attract a lot of notice, because he looked like many of the little respectable men about Malvern Rd where I lived. He was said to be a draper. I was familiar with the word, but asked my mother, who made comparison to one of our local shops which sold men's and children's clothing rather than women's clothing.

Mussolini has been caught again, and the Russians are shelling Berlin. Everything collapses at once, as if the whole second phase of the War in Europe is condensed into a few days. I am confused about the word Bunker and am told it is a huge cellar with fortifications against bombing and often deep underground. Hitler is in it with Eva Braun.

And then before the Russians can get him, he kills himself and Eva Braun, but nobody finds his body and no remains of him were ever identified. It all seems very strange to my parents, and my father speculates on where he might have gone, and the newspaper says that the Russian soldiers who first found him must know what happened to his body.

Admiral Doenitz is made the German Chancellor. I can remember thinking 'why does Germany need to have another Chancellor — it is all over when Hitler is dead, or is he dead? Mussolini has been hung in Italy, Goering and Goebbels have committed suicide, but I have never heard of Admiral Doenitz. The German army has surrendered to Eisenhower, and in Berlin, to the Russians.

And then it is VE day in early May.

And does this look as if the Japanese will fold up as their Allies in Europe have done?

The loss in Europe seems to have not the slightest effect on them, as if this war was quite different from the one in Europe, and early surrender is of no consideration. My father and Uncle Basil are sure that taking the whole of the Japanese Islands is going to require fighting because of the huge losses that occurred at Iwo Jima and were happening now in Okinawa.

Okinawa

You might imagine me in that early part of 45, when Okinawa means new maps everywhere. It is the focus of the war. Two or three papers today, Herald, Sun – and the big brown radio often had something new.

The initial American landings went well until they approached areas the Japanese had prepared to defend. The landings on the beaches were hardly opposed, because of the elaborate tactical defences at the ridges that crossed the Island. In Okinawa they were going to sell each life dearly. The Newsreels from Okinawa rolled on for many weeks, and this left the adults thinking that the war in Japan itself would be similarly long, fierce and costly.

It is happening between ridges and rock - full of caves, and the enemy know them all. When I saw the bigger map of this natural fortress against the South Island of Japan, Okinawa had to be won before the invasion of Japan itself.

On the ground an attempt to take the next step finds the Americans to be under heavy fire, an easy target for the defenders. We heard the soldiers on both sides had hand grenades and rifles. American bombs were dropped but targets were underground. US tanks were doing well until there was mud everywhere. The Americans advanced one cave at a time, 'blowing them up' as they went.

In May the radio reported fierce fighting at sea and in the caves – a huge loss of life on both sides. The taking of Okinawa was still happening, great loss of ships and planes were reported daily.

Back in Creswick Street we were frightened — if this was what it was like at Okinawa, what would taking Japan be like? Further parts of the war looked bad ahead. There was a sense of everyone at home being shocked because we couldn't see the future. So close to Japan but being killed by the thousand. The shock was a bit like the bombing of Darwin.

Reg and Basil

So, it is no wonder then that the brothers Reg and Basil sitting over our small-grate wood fire (one of them would periodically stand holding the mantel piece or even leaning on it to warm other parts of his body – it was a very cold house in winter) the residents of Creswick St were pessimistic about the Pacific War. The locals were talking grimly, "Soon we will see how they like it when it is all going on in their country", anticipating that anybody who could carry a weapon would be defending each yard of Japan. They said that the occupation forces would have to be enormous.

This week was a climax to the battle of Okinawa. When they finally had the opportunity of being at the south side of the island and surrounding the Japanese defenders, the engagements continued until the battle was declared over at the beginning of the last week in June.

In the air the Japanese had lost too many planes, even though there were a couple more kamikaze raids they were not of the strength of the previous effort and the defences against them more capable.

The airfields on the north and centre of the island were being repaired and the Allied planes were gathering there. That was not to stop a two engine Japanese bomber landing there on its belly (after its four or five companions had been shot down) and a small number of infantry men jumping out and putting bombs in nearby parked planes and refuelling equipment.

School again

Kent Street side of the school.

At school I was surprised to learn that we were to have an examination in the middle of the year to see how we were progressing. I always tackled any examination as well as I could; they came as a challenge where I could show my best. But despite coming in the top few in science, my other marks, particularly algebra, geometry, Latin, and history were low. I was told I was to be changed from 1A to 1B and that some of the good students from 1B were to have an opportunity to be in 1A.

My parents who thought I was doing reasonably well, were astounded. They noted that my science mark and place were even better than expected but were told that my other marks were really down. I don't know what my parents said to each other, but for the first time my father showed an interest in my schoolwork and inquired about my homework (I didn't do homework).

This resulted in my textbooks being brought out, including my Latin text. I most remember doing the algebra and Latin with my father, and my mother taking an interest in the geometry.

It turned out that my father knew long streams of Latin prayers that he mostly did not understand and anyway wanted to forget. He had been an Altar boy with a Catholic upbringing, that for him had become a disaster after his father died when he was in primary school. He remembered getting into much trouble; I knew that two of his father's sisters were nuns and he was irritable if they were mentioned, and I now know that even thinking about them was included in his avoidance. But he could say Latin the right way. I can still remember the book started: 'Discipuli picturam spectate'.

I was becoming acquainted with my new form 1B, the second-string class of what we would now call Year 7. I was almost eleven and a half. Miss Jones was the roll-call teacher, she reminded me of Miss Kell from Grade 4. She taught Art and I was already acquainted with her, but I was totally previously unnoticed by her at art lessons. She was cheerful and seemed to be in a good mood most of the time. It was a class of almost double the number of girls to boys. Many of them had been in my primary school class for the previous six years.

One issue that intruded, and Miss Jones remarked on, as if it was something she would tell everybody, that her extraordinary boys were five called Geoffrey, and that now there was a sixth. It reflected the popularity of the name in 1932 – 33 of course, as well as coincidence, and with the parents of those in 1B.

I was still focused tightly on the war. The question was the invasion of the Japanese Home Islands. They were said to have two million soldiers, and that every adult person on the islands would be armed and trained. I was still preoccupied by the deaths of Iwo Jima and Okinawa. It was reported that one Japanese leader Suzuki had repeated that they would fight to the last man before unconditionally surrendering. I was fully aware of the import of this from Churchill's position in Europe.

There was a lull in the war at the end of June and early July. Everybody knew the American pattern of rapidly building airfields on captive Islands was going on apace. Before the invasion of Japan itself could take place the Japanese air-force and naval capacity would have to be hugely diminished.

Bombing raids of Japan not only continued from aircraft carriers, but I was not surprised in the middle of July when Flying Fortresses were taking off from Okinawa to bomb Japanese airfields. The big battleships, and even some of the smaller ones from the US Navy, were shelling 'the Japanese war effort' as the Newsreels called it.

In both Swanson and Collins St Melbourne, the newsreel theatres continually ran the latest newsreel: dramatic highlighting voice, with echoing tones that still can run around in my very old head. These weeks they were exceptionally busy. There was now a British aircraft carrier off Japan, and its planes attacked Japanese airfields. You had to wait in the queue, pay your sixpence. Yet you could watch it twice if you wanted to. Still sixpence was two big ice-cream cones.

My mother was very emotional at this stage of the war. Not only could she see that a huge number of people would die or be maimed as permanent casualties of war, but she said that now they had found that Japanese cities would burn to the point of creating fire storms, the people who were just followers and "not all like Tojo," (my class all knew Junishi and his mother as fairly ordinary) and would lose their homes and relatives and be terribly burnt. She said that this was to happen to cities all over Japan and that she couldn't see any end to it. She had been horrified by Belsen, but her horror here was not about something that had already happened, but about what was about to happen. I became quite affected by her feelings and watched the papers ever more closely.

I found I could read Miss Jones' expressions and was not in awe of her, as I was Miss Lindner. I would sometimes interrupt with an answer, and even when admonished, I knew she was following what I was up to and didn't mind it at all. This helped me get over some of my classroom withdrawal and I felt better about being in school.

This time was like waiting for D Day. You knew D Day was going to come eventually and that it had taken a huge amount of planning and secrecy, and Uncle Basil said it was going to be the biggest invasion of a country there had ever been. I was confused about this because I knew the Japanese were hard fighters particularly close up and they had an enormous army, but I had a sense of the size of Japan compared with the bulk of Europe and America. And the Americans couldn't do anything but the absolute strongest invasion. But like D Day it would never come. General MacArthur actually said on the news during that week about it was going to be a huge invasion.

Margaret is six, August 4

A different weekend, as Margaret was to turn 6 on August 4th and it was a Saturday. It was a reminder day too about how long we had been at war. Early August at Creswick St, the jonquils were in flower and the few daffodils were to follow within days, the almond blossom came before the plums and apples. My father still worked on Saturday morning. My mother's friends, the Livingstone 'girls' Ada and Jessie would come, with Ada's niece Helen about the same age, some of the local girls, and this time with her being at school, some school friends. Cupcakes and an iced sponge cake with candles and a cream filling were central to such parties. Fresh bread and butter with 'hundreds and thousands' were cut to triangular quarters, and they too were mandatory. These were the days when all such items were cooked freshly at home, but the green or red jelly had to be taken to the Malvern Rd dairy to be put into their fridge for it to set and keep for the party.

School and work on the Monday morning. I ate lunch at school and left for home at 'ten to four in the afternoon' coming through the back gate across the cracked deserted tennis courts and into the back garden.

The Atom Bomb

My mother immediately caught my attention and said, "they have dropped a new bomb on Japan — an Atom bomb. Just one bomb has wiped out a whole Japanese city."

My mother was not excited by this but more serious and puzzled. I heard what she said and was astonished. She said that "first it was about, … Belsen and now this new horror." She had a sense of WW2 being absolutely necessary, but a different sense about WW1, yet "The Kaiser had to be stopped", she said.

I was shocked for a bit, but then knew I was frightened that such a bomb existed. It would not be long until my father came home and then the 6 o'clock news on 3DB. We always listened to it. I wanted to find out as much as I could about this Atom Bomb and what had happened. My father was spot on time at ten to five.

He was alert rather than tired or irritable. 'It's a 'very big bomb' he said, or words to that effect. 'And only one did it all.' The Herald said 'Atomic bomb' rather than Atom bomb. The main thing I remember was that 'the atom was split' and this had made it so enormous.

'This is going to make a difference to the war,' my father said.

'The whole city was flattened completely, and there were fires and tens of thousands of people were killed,' the 6 o'clock news said.

The other item that stuck in my mind was 'the mushroom cloud'. My Imagination of this was accurate, but I would find out the next day that this was unbelievably bigger than my imaginings, because when next day the news said the mushroom cloud rose to fifty-thousand-feet, and I knew Mount Everest was twenty-nine-thousand feet. I started to think in a real scale about what had happened.

The bomb days

We didn't have a science lesson that day, and I wanted to know what Miss Lindner thought; she was the one person who would tell us all about it.

The children had a lot to say about the atomic bomb the next day. I was imagining one being dropped on the middle of Melbourne and what damage it would do. Miss Jones seemed to not know any more about it than we did. My father that evening repeated from the newspaper that we were at the beginning of The Atomic Age.

The children were in various stages of shock particularly echoing how their parents were reacting, fear that it could come to our doorstep now that the bomb existed. Photos appeared in the Sun of the mushroom cloud. Articles on the nuclear process were there for all to read. At our house there was anxiety for the future as well as my mother's high concern of all those who now suffered in Japan. A whole city. Gone in an instant.

Miss Lindner did much to keep us children calm and informed.

On the following day during the science lesson, she was calm and matter of fact about what the scientists had discovered. I was fascinated by her description of the process leading up to the chain reaction. The two broken parts of the atom would weigh less than the original, and this mass had been turned into energy.

'So,' she explained, 'the bomb must have been made by putting two pieces of uranium 235 together quickly to set it off.'

She was to teach us about alpha, beta and gamma rays too. I saw her looking at me as she was doing various parts of this explanation. She let me ask questions, instead of holding the palm of her hand at me to indicate that I must let others ask questions too.

The 'painfully slow war' had speeded up even more, because on the Thursday, another atom bomb was dropped on a Japanese city called Nagasaki. It was said to be a naval centre with docks and shipping.

Later, I wandered to the wood heap to pick up chips of wood and cut some more to light the fire; this was my job every afternoon for the winter and most of spring. It was cut into blocks about a foot long that had to be split with an axe. One trick to split it was to get the axe stuck into the block, and then turn it all over and land the back of the axe heavily on the chopping block.

I enjoyed lighting the fire, because the house really needed it as it was poorly insulated, but more, because there was some deep satisfaction, even pride in doing it that came in a mysterious way that I could never explain.

Sometimes I had some briquettes to burn or even some Wonthaggi black coal, but the house was small enough that the heat seemed to spread around the house. The flames could get going and would often go up the chimney.

* *

The ceremony at school. At some stage there was a very large formal ceremony at school, all students gathered on the asphalt in the front of the school, red white and blue flags on high poles, particularly Union Jack, hymns were sung including 'God save the King 'and 'There will always be an England', and there were tributes, with names of families who had lost someone serving — some children identified as having lost a father.

I noticed where Creswick Street with 26 houses, had many who served and were injured or POW, while adjacent Aintree Road seemed to have more than their share of those who did not return.

I watched the VE celebrating searchlights all coming up from the Melbourne area - we watched from the tennis courts.

(Much later we would have a gathering to watch the Sputnik, 4 October 1957.)

* *

In the later part of the year, my teacher was Mr Jock Pedlow a tall thin older man with a red face. I was sitting in the front row of the class, and he always seemed to be watching me closely, with an expectation of what we were learning. On this day I had left important books outside the classroom and Mr Pedlow waved an indication for me to go and get them, this meant I had to stand and pass him as I went to the door – he whacked me very hard across the back with his strap. It was painful but I did not make much of it at home until I had a bath and my father saw the long black bruise across my back. This led to my parents going to friends on the school committee and that strap was never seen again. (We now know that as I am a 'diagnosed bleeder', this may have multiplied the effect.)

> Apparently Jock Pedlow was well known for his leather strap with a wooden handle. At lunch time he would stalk the grounds. If you were standing near a discarded lunch paper, you got belted.

The toilet block from the gravel sports ground.

End of the war

The news reported parties going on in the streets. Back at school some of the boys were boasting about a big party in the main street of our municipal centre – Glenferrie Rd, Malvern. They had been kissing girls, they boasted. 'Skiting' we called it. They didn't talk about the war or 'the bomb'.

My mother's reaction was on the 'Surely it must stop soon' theme — essentially that what was happening now must change everybody's view.

By the weekend we knew that the Japanese were saying they wanted peace and were going to accept the ultimatum from 'the Potsdam meeting' some weeks ago.

The fighting and bombing seemed to have stopped, but we heard that the Russians, who had only declared war on Japan on the Thursday, were defeating the Japanese army in Manchuria. Then on the following Wednesday it was announced worldwide that the war was over.

This included the Japanese telling their own people it was over and the beginning of what this would mean for them. It would be called VP Day August 15th. We went home from school early that day.

There was relief obvious in almost everybody. Also, there was a strange feeling as if everything was done to have the war over, and now it was over — what?

What was to happen to us?

My father's reaction was one of preoccupation with the end of the war, and what that might mean for us. With his job making parts for the US forces and the live shells I had seen, he had been getting more 'overtime' that had kept up our payments on the tennis courts, and this would come to an end, but the courts were too cracked up to be playable, and, as they were, would not generate any income at all.

Aftermath

Marg remembers the soldier relatives visiting now, before being demobbed to various parts of Australia, the WA cousins Cliff and Doris, their brother-in-law Bert Todhunter. Lindsay Tacon returned to Creswick St as did others further down the street, Army, Navy, Airforce uniforms.

The Scarlett family's eldest boy Charlie had been captured by the Japanese in Ambon in 1942 and his whereabouts were very uncertain: indeed, whether he was dead or alive. He was found in a prison camp on that Island, and we heard he was coming back after 'the hospital' had made him well enough to live outside. My mother explained that they were worked and starved, and had diseases like malaria, and, if they gave them normal food, it would just turn to gas and make them vomit, and it all had to be done very slowly.

Some weeks later I saw Charlie in Creswick St. I was shocked because of his skin being a strange yellow and looking like crumpled paper or thin cardboard. My mother explained that Charlie's yellow colouring was partly due to a medicine called Atebrin that was used against malaria. You could see all his bones, even the bones of his face under his skin. I was aware his family were praying and crying and giving thanks for him being alive. His brother Donny (my age) said Charlie had only a very small amount of rice to eat each day. He was very thin. It was strange to think that when I saw him many months later when he had come to see if any of the Tennis Courts were playable, I recognised which one of the older brothers he was from years earlier.

Even when my father saw him about a week later, he was shocked and realised how he had no idea how badly they had been treated. He wasn't so sympathetic about one of his own cousins who had been in the Military Hospital Heidelberg in Eastern Melbourne for unspecified ailments, who had boasted about his ability to go to hospital if it suited him at the time, and how he was inventing a building board that curved around corners and would make him a fortune.

There was a lot of talk about Repatriation and helping the soldiers to come back to civilian life, and a man my father knew from his earlier life was to be made Minister for Post-war Reconstruction.

That November after my father had taken an interest in my homework and preparation for exams; I had the best mark in the IB class by a big margin and was promoted for next year to 2A.

1945 to 1951

From science teachers to Medicine.

My dreamy withdrawal from lessons however seemed to be set in, except for science. I was accepted for Melbourne Boys High School for 1947 but in the lowest class 3H. The English teacher Mr Williamson wrote to my parents along the lines that my schoolwork had a huge discrepancy to my measured IQ. I was sent for a vocational guidance test that told my parents I could do anything I wanted to, including things mechanical. (I was always the one who handed my father the implement he wanted.)

But this meant I was to be promoted to 4C the following year. This year might have been better, but I was heavily bullied by an older boy with a congenitally deformed arm, and the science teacher became very ill and was not replaced; we were often simply supervised by the PT teacher.

The inspiring teacher

It was not until the middle of 5th form (Year 11; 1949) that I was to have a chemistry teacher who was inspiring; even though I had done my dreamy withdrawal in the first term, I had observed the periodic table on the wall in great detail and was fascinated by it. I listened to the atomic structure, and then read much about the periodic table in the library. In the second term I lifted my score from the thirties to the seventies.

Jack Stove was a young teacher and would suddenly ask me a question when I wasn't looking. He liked my answers. I knew he was watching me and interested to see what I could do. The practical work done as a twosome with another student was very much hands on, and I found I had to take the lead in this. I kept up my extra-curricular reading and found that I was getting to know these atoms, and there was a strong sense of how they would combine with each other and form useful molecules. It was as if they were like people but much more consistent. In the matriculation year in 1950, he would start to talk about a chemical, – and flash – and he would go straight on with the lesson.

He encouraged me quietly but precisely, and I took the mood of it from him in a manner that my peers would not rise to.

This was the re-education experience I had not had since Mrs Thompson in fifth grade. About June in 1950 my father came home on his alternate Thursday evening from work (pay day) and ruminated after he'd had a few drinks (not many because the pubs closed at six o'clock and he only drank once a fortnight) about what he would do if he won Tatts (the legendary lottery). I said that if he did, I would do Medicine. At that time there was no support for financially disadvantaged students doing expensive six-year courses. Nothing of this sort had ever been broached before, even in my mother's musings about bank managers or navy officers.

The effect on both of my parents was of the 'slapped in the face by a wet fish' variety. My father went to the local doctor to talk about it. I said that I was not doing Physics or a Maths and that this precluded me. My parents found there was some talk about the Menzies Government commencing a Commonwealth Scholarship in 1951.

Some months later I realised that I could get the marks to get in, except for the required prerequisites. I decided to take myself to the Faculty of Medicine and talk to the Secretary, Mr Elford. I often wonder what he thought about a sixteen-year-old boy of doubtful maturity coming so see him wanting to commence the intensely competitive First Year Medicine. (They regularly failed 'a majority of the Year', this raised such an outcry at the time. Later they changed the name to Pre-medicine without compromising their standards). He was kind and courteous and listened to what I said on my own behalf. He took down my details and told me it would depend on what my marks were in the Matriculation (HSC) examination. I thanked him and worked hard. Very hard.

I achieved a Second-Class Honour in Chemistry 'after having done only four of the five questions required' and came first in Biology — so I set out on my quest for a license to do hard work.

Writing this on New Year's Day 2014, 1950 seems a long way away.

Looking back, the war years and the education of one boy. My Gardiner School years went from early excitement about education right through the War to the Atom Bomb and the aftermath.

It gave me a view into the ups and downs of the adult world under stress. A lesson well learned; the strong bonds of extended family, the role of school teachers and their particular ups and downs.

It made me very aware of the effects of bullying by peers, and some negative teacher influence on children, and opened the door to the brilliance of other teachers.

And the door to my day dreaming adventures was pushed to the forefront, increasing as an intense reaction of survival in year 6.

And — the ongoing discovery of science, and love of long-term learning. Moving along a direction, to where it was my own enquiry and decision to one day study medicine, with a deep wish to be involved in a caring and scientific profession.

Melbourne Boys High School was also to contribute.

Personal excerpts

Uncle Frank Hartley had stayed in Australia after his kidney surgery and recovery and was promoted to a teaching job in the Navy, training young recruits in special skills in the mechanics of the engines that drive big ships. He left the Navy at the end of the war.

Basil and Poppy Rickarby. Poppy managed the only frock shop in Tooronga and Basil continued as Richmond Station Master until they retired and eventually built their home at Christmas Hills.

Uncle Joe Justins, 1876 to 1960. He was a neighbour and school mate of the Skead family. Joe was a Richmond footballer up until 1903. He had a Post Office career. Later he became a director of Gold Mining companies. During the depression he was instrumental in rescuing the tennis courts cooperative.

Reg, Freda and Margaret

Repatriating the tennis courts: my father's scheme over the next three years was to build the tennis courts with furnace ash rolled, and then a layer of finer ash, then coarse red brick dust followed by fine. This would build en-tous-cas courts that would drain off any amount of rain and be playable in a variety of weathers.

We started the following year by cementing bluestone blocks, one deep, in a low wall around the edge of the courts to contain all this. By 1949 we had all of them finished, but tennis never had the popularity that it had pre-war.

However, by the 50s Reg was a popular children's tennis coach and the courts were busy again. And Reg was able to borrow money to buy his first car in 1951, a Holden. In 1963, by the time Reg turned 60, they sold the courts went on a world trip and retired to Croydon to live near Geoff and family.

In 1951 Margaret went on to MLC for six years, and then completed the occupational therapy course in 1959.

Story still ongoing, Christmas, 2024

We thank the Gardiner Central School Facebook, for the use of school pictures.

Margaret in grade 2, second row right, three in.

2025

Aged 91 this year, Geoff is still working on poetry.

His earlier poetry books were written under the pseudonym:

QB WILLOWBY

Melbourne So Far Away, 1976, "with a hug of Capricorn air" ISBN 0949741 00 0

Motley Leaves, 2017, "I come from a far star at my own speed" ISBN978-0-9586836-1-6

Roses in the Rain, 2021, "a farrago of Willowby verse" ISBN 978-0-646-84205-9

******

And under the pseudonym:

THOMAS SKEAD

Zen is Development was first published in 1996, "a personal journey through allegorical ox-herding imagery" ISBN – 0- 9586836 0 3

A revised paperback version was published in 2023, "poetic presentation" ISBN 978-0-6453599-1-6

******

For his medical articles, search 'Dr Geoff Rickarby' on Google.

Margaret and Geoffrey Rickarby

www.ingramcontent.com/pod-product-compliance
Lightning Source LLC
Chambersburg PA
CBRC091958300426
44109CB00007BA/163